A BASIC HISTORY OF

THE OLD SOUTH

WENDELL HOLMES STEPHENSON

Professor of History
University of Oregon

AN ANVIL ORIGINAL

under the general editorship of

LOUIS L. SNYDER

D. VAN NOSTRAND COMPANY, INC.

PRINCETON, NEW JERSEY

TORONTO   LONDON

To Robert Lewis Stephenson and
Margaret Stephenson Moore
Brother and Sister of a Younger Generation

VAN NOSTRAND REGIONAL OFFICES:
New York, Chicago, San Francisco

D. VAN NOSTRAND COMPANY, LTD., *London*

D. VAN NOSTRAND COMPANY (Canada), LTD., *Toronto*

PRINTED IN THE UNITED STATES OF AMERICA

PREFACE

It is easier to write a long book than a short one. The first draft of the present volume's textual portion ran to twice the length of the published version. The selecting and compressing processes removed many sections in their entirety and emaciated others beyond recognition. Readers who are familiar with the whole panorama of the Old South's history will marvel—along with the writer—at important aspects of the subject that were not admitted to the story and at the cavalier treatment of others that received only a paragraph or a sentence. The two hundred and fifty years that elapsed between the founding of Jamestown and the beginning of the Civil War were chock-full of significant persons, events, and movements to which a group of associated scholars, in a coöperative work in progress, are devoting a million two hundred and fifty thousand words. There are about thirty thousand in the present publication, designed chiefly for readers who may profit from some essentials compressed into brief compass.

Apart from the hundreds of writers who have pioneered in Southern history, the writer's main obligation is to his wife Hildagarde, who patiently shared the drudgery of typing, copyreading, and proofing. He is grateful also to publishers who graciously permitted reproduction of copyrighted accounts (acknowledged specifically in footnotes) in the documentary part of the book; and to Dr. Jane Carson of Colonial Williamsburg, Inc., for verification of material unavailable locally. A few paragraphs in Chapter 7 have been adapted from the writer's "Antebellum New Orleans as an Agricultural Focus," *Agricultural History*, XV (October, 1941), pp. 166-167.

Eugene, Oregon   WENDELL HOLMES STEPHENSON
October, 1959

TABLE OF CONTENTS

Part One—A BASIC HISTORY OF THE OLD SOUTH

— 1 —

THE LAND AND THE PEOPLE

The South: From Geographical Expression to Self-Conscious Unity. The South is a geographical location, a group of factors that differentiated the region and its inhabitants from other sections of the United States, and a state of mind to which those factors gave rise. In the colonial period "the South" was merely a geographical expression. Inhabitants of the colonies from Delaware and Maryland south to Georgia were not even Americans. They were Englishmen for the most part, with accretions of Germans, Scotch-Irish, French Huguenots, and a few others as the seventeenth century faded into the eighteenth. Native Indians inhabited all the commonwealths; Spaniards occupied the borderland provinces of Florida and Texas, and Frenchmen the colony of Louisiana, all of which would eventually become parts of the South.

Gradually in the eighteenth century the wilderness and the melting pot made Europeans into Americans; and just as imperceptibly in the years from the Revolution to the Civil War, Northern and Southern Americans became aware of differences that brought clash and conflict in constitutional and legislative bodies, in newspapers and magazines, pamphlets and petitions. A few of these differences were apparent in the late colonial and Revolutionary periods, and they became more obvious in the years from 1787 to the Missouri Compromise; but a self-conscious South that struggled to maintain minority rights was a product of the decades from 1820 to 1860.

Difficulty in Defining and Locating the South.
The concept of the South as the region below Mason and
Dixon's line is quite traditional; yet such a location is in
many respects inadequate. Only in a limited sense was
that historic line the northern boundary of the South; it
eventually separated the slaveholding from the nonslaveholding states. Yet four border commonwealths—Delaware, Maryland, Kentucky, and Missouri—were not
sufficiently Southern to abandon the Union in 1861; the
western part of the Old Dominion refused to follow Virginia into the Confederacy; a large mountainous region
was Southern chiefly in latitude; and in every Southern
state there was Unionist sentiment as secession became
a reality.

Should such cities as Baltimore, Wheeling, Cincinnati,
Louisville, and St. Louis be classified as Northern or
Southern depending upon their location with respect to
Mason and Dixon's line? The population of each, in fact,
manifested diversity of view. There was considerable
Southern sympathy and sentiment in parts of Northern
border states, particularly in Ohio, Indiana, and Illinois.
Southerners made notable contributions to the institutional and social order of the Old Northwest; and tobacco, a Southern staple, was a minor element in the
economic life of the region north of the Ohio River. The
great Mississippi was a channel of trade and communication between the upper and lower parts of the valley.
It becomes apparent at once that Mason and Dixon's
line was essentially artificial.

**Zones of Land Mark the Northern and Western
Limits of the South.** The northern limit of the South
is a zone of land rather than a distinct line. As the ante-
bellum visitor traveled north, the South imperceptibly
merged into the North. The distinguishing features of the
landscape, the percentage of Negroes in the population,
the way of life with the social and economic factors upon
which it was based, the attitude of the people upon controversial and sectional issues—these and other factors
that made the Old South Southern gradually disappeared.
The transition was so evolutionary that the wayfarer
might travel two or three hundred miles before the
change seemed complete. Likewise, as he traveled west,

the transition was no more abrupt. Somewhere in Texas, Arkansas, the Indian country that became Oklahoma, and Missouri, the South met the West, but the traveler had difficulty in determining when he passed from one region to the other.

Southern Diversity. Whether the geographical South is defined narrowly or liberally, it is a vast region. From Chesapeake Bay to the Rio Grande is fifteen hundred miles; from southwestern Missouri to the Florida Everglades is approximately a thousand. The British Isles, France, Portugal, Spain, and Italy could be superimposed on a map of the slaveholding area and there would still be more than enough room for all of the New England and Middle Atlantic states. It follows logically that the South's human and physical geography were greatly diversified: that it comprised a variety of soil, climate, and population. The Cotton Kingdom occupied a considerable portion of the lower or deep South, though every state from South Carolina to Texas contained much land not devoted to the staple. Much of the upper South from Maryland to Missouri found its most important money crop in tobacco. The line of demarcation between the Cotton and Tobacco Kingdoms was as artificial as that between the North and the South; though probably the transition between the upper and the lower South was somewhat more abrupt, especially in the tramontane region, than was that between Yankeedom and Dixie. The Scotch-Irish in the Piedmont of South Atlantic commonwealths had little in common with the French in Louisiana. Lowlanders in South Carolina and hill men of Arkansas differed in more than economic status. Even in the same state, people often attained little accord. There were perennial contests between New Orleans and the country parishes of Louisiana, and civil strife between Tidewater and upcountry folk frequently threatened the domestic tranquillity of Virginia and the Carolinas.

One must be cautious, because of this great diversity, in the use of such generalities as "Southern opinion" and "Southern attitude." Neither homogeneity nor heterogeneity followed state boundary lines. Sections or regions were much more significant, socially, economically, or culturally, than states. Perhaps only in the realm of politics and local policy were states as divisions or entities of any great importance.

Fundamental and Enduring Factors That Made the South Southern. In spite of diversity, there were forces of a fundamental and enduring nature that made the South Southern and its inhabitants Southerners. These factors operated to develop an attitude of nationalism that culminated, perhaps avoidably, in a four-year conflict for Southern independence. Some of them have not entirely disappeared by the middle of the twentieth century.

A basic force in moulding a Southern consciousness was the presence of Negroes in large numbers. The institution of slavery evolved in part to provide a permanent source of labor supply, but slave codes were enacted to assure a social system that would guarantee "white supremacy"; in short, as the late Ulrich B. Phillips expressed it, to make and keep the South a white man's country. That this attitude survived the emancipation of the slave—even to the middle of the twentieth century in the minds of some white Southerners—is indicative of its fundamental character. The fact that the myth of "white supremacy" has been exploded does not affect the historical importance of the concept.

Phillips' "Central Theme" of Southern history is worth quoting even though some disagreement exists as to its centrality. The South, he wrote in the 1920's, "is a land with a unity despite its diversity, with a people having common joys and common sorrows, and, above all, as to the white folk a people with a common resolve indomitably maintained—that it shall be and remain a white man's country." Whether this consciousness is "expressed with the frenzy of a demagogue or maintained with a patrician's quietude," it "is the cardinal test of a Southerner and the central theme of Southern history" (*American Historical Review,* October, 1928, XXXIV, 31). The ancient error of Negro inferiority still persists in some quarters, but historically speaking, ancient error may be more important than present truth.

The agricultural way of life, or at least way of work, was another factor that helped to make the South Southern. Through the colonial and ante-bellum periods, and

until the advent of the New South in the decades following Reconstruction, the South was almost wholly agrarian. Even after the Southern industrial trek the region
was still predominantly rural. While the Old South did
not concentrate upon the great staples—cotton, tobacco,
rice, and sugar cane—as much as tradition would have
us believe, still there was sufficient emphasis to give character and direction to much of the economic thinking.
The Old South possessed its advocates of industry, pioneers who demonstrated that manufacturing was feasible,
but their preachments did not disturb the fundamental
agrarian philosophy of a predominantly rural population.

This agrarian emphasis not only promoted rurality
but also scattered homesteads and decentralized government. The colonial assembly of the Old Dominion passed
acts creating towns, many of which existed only on paper. South Carolina, it is true, developed as a city state,
with Charleston as a commercial and cultural center as
well as a political capital; but it was the exception rather
than the rule. Savannah, Mobile, New Orleans, and Natchez became thriving commercial centers, but their
commercialism did not destroy the essential rural characteristic of the South which survived Civil War and Reconstruction. Under such conditions local government
became a sacred institution, individualism a pronounced
attribute, and democracy a noble ideal.

Climate was another contributing factor. A prolonged
growing season, varying from six months at the northern
extremity to nine on the Gulf Coast, encouraged production of the Southern staples. The length of the summers rather than unusual heat distinguished the South.
The region was not affected by such extremes of temperature as the North. A survey based upon Weather
Bureau statistics reveals that when other sections are
sweltering with maximum July temperatures, they are
three degrees warmer than the hottest midsummer days
in the South; and when January blizzards harass the
country, Northern and Western cities have temperatures
twenty-four degrees lower than Southern towns. Within
the South, winter temperatures vary markedly from Missouri to Texas and from Kentucky to Mississippi. There
are few killing frosts along the Gulf Coast, and only sel

dom are residents of southern Louisiana and Georgia treated to the novelty of a sprinkling of snow. Annual rainfall is excessive on the plains and plentiful everywhere, though summers are occasionally punctuated with drouths. Pelting rains pack the soil and result in flooded streams. Summer skies are characterized by clouds as fleecy as the cotton staple, except when those of darker hue bring showers without the customary middle-western thunderstorms. The monotony of long summers produces a languidness that causes the leisurely, easygoing Southerner to work with less drive than his Northern neighbor, albeit his way of work may yield tangible results.

Climate and agriculture were contributing factors in a chain of events that resulted in Negro labor. The traditional view that Southern whites could not stand hard work under the summer sun has gone the way of other myths, for there were farmers who did their own labor from the seventeenth to the twentieth century. The Negro thrived in hot weather, he was largely immune to malaria so prevalent in the swamps from South Carolina to Louisiana, and he was useful in performing routine labor in large-scale agriculture. He might acquire skills that accentuated his value in town and country.

Slaveholding contributed to the development of a small leisured class of planters who were relieved of toil but not of responsibility. A country gentleman ideal arose, in fact as well as in fiction, which made an art of living and relegated business to a subordinate position in the Southern way of life. This cultured class, always a small minority, held political office out of proportion to its numbers, patronized the arts, and formed a caste which was, however, in no way closed to the ambitious farmer or the professional man. Below the great planter class there were small slaveholders, prosperous farmers, and other sturdy yeomen who occupied an important position in the human geography of the South. There were, in addition, poor whites in every state, whose economic and social status made them determined opponents of the Negro. Slaves were everywhere the "mudsills" of society, ever oppressed but often treated kindly.

Free Negroes had few special privileges in an area where white men believed in white supremacy.

These several factors, intangible as some of them seem, eventually operated to give white Southerners a sense of unity which Southern diversity did not actually justify. Southerners, some consciously and others unconsciously, came to think of their section as the South and of themselves as Southerners. In formulating this mental status, criticism from the outside, especially after 1830, played a significant role.

The Face of the Land. The first physical division of the future South to receive settlers, whether English, Spanish, or French, was the Coastal Plain, stretching from the head of Delaware Bay to the Rio Grande. Occupying almost a third of the area, the Plain—and the Mississippi River Embayment—includes varying proportions of all Old South states. The interior boundary is the fall line, so called because for much of its length it intersects rivers flowing into the Atlantic or the Gulf of Mexico at falls or rapids that became sites of cities and towns. The Tidewater region, as the Plain bordering the Atlantic came to be called, varies in width from a hundred to two hundred miles in its southwesterly sweep to Georgia. The fall line or "zone" bends sharply into central Alabama, where it turns northwest to meet the Tennessee. West of the Mississippi it curves to the southwest to include in Embayment and Plain the southeastern corner of Missouri, eastern and southern Arkansas, the southeastern fringe of Oklahoma, and eastern Texas.

The rest of the South consists of plateau, valley, and mountain land. A hypothetical traveler leaving Norfolk for Missouri or Arkansas traversed several physical divisions before he arrived at his destination. Beyond the Tidewater he reached the rolling and rugged Piedmont Province, lying between the fall line and the Blue Ridge Mountains and extending from Pennsylvania to eastern Alabama. As the traveler crossed the Piedmont he saw the Blue Ridge in the distance, shrouded in a bluish haze. They widened from fifteen or twenty miles in Maryland and Virginia to a hundred or more in western North Carolina, eastern Tennessee, and northern Georgia. The wayfarer could penetrate them at Potomac or James River watergaps and emerge into a beautiful Valley and Ridge, hedged on the west by the Allegheny-Cumberland Front of West Virginia, eastern Kentucky and Tennessee, and northern Alabama.

A much-traveled route from the Valley to backwoods and Bluegrass lay through Cumberland Gap at the intersection of Kentucky, Tennessee, and Virginia. The Gap led the traveler to the Interior Low Plateaus of central Kentucky and Tennessee and northern Alabama. Within the division he discovered two Bluegrass regions of considerable importance in Southern history, the Lexington Plain and the Nashville Basin. Crossing the northern Mississippi Embayment, the traveler reached the Ozark Plateau of Missouri, Arkansas, and Oklahoma. The Ozarks and Interior Low Plateaus straddle the Embayment like huge saddlebags.

Southern Sectionalism and Southern Nationalism. Western Europeans who migrated to South Atlantic commonwealths were not unlike those who arrived in their northern counterparts. Inhabitants of the Southern area who participated in the establishment of new frontier areas in the West approximated frontiersmen who helped to subdue any Western wilderness, valley, or plain. A considerable part of Southern history is therefore American history or Western history. Southern sectionalism emerged slowly, reaching fruition in the years between the Missouri Compromise and the Mexican War. Southern nationalism—the movement for an independent South—reached climactic proportions in the last antebellum decade.

2

CHESAPEAKE COUNTRY

In the colonial period of American history, a half-dozen commonwealths were planted south of Mason and Dixon's line. Geographical factors, surveying expeditions, and the whim of monarchs determined their boundaries, gloriously indefinite in pioneer years. St. Mary's and Annapolis, Jamestown and Williamsburg, New Bern and Edenton, Charles Town and Savannah, served as colonial capitals; governors, assemblies, and courts met to make laws, levy taxes, and administer justice. Except for the few functions of local government, life and labor had a way of ignoring provincial boundaries. Economy and society depended largely upon soil, climate, means of transportation, character of the population—and mere chance.

Southern Societies in the Colonial Period. Chesapeake Country, Carolina-Georgia Lowlands, and Back Country were more realistic areas than the colonial enterprises established along the South Atlantic seaboard. Beyond the limits of North America, a society and economy developed in the West Indies, where sugar cane and slavery provided contrasts and comparisons and in some instances direct influences.

Geography of the Chesapeake Country. When John Smith, Edward Maria Wingfield, and their associates arrived in Chesapeake Bay in 1607, their concept of that great expanse of water and the land that surrounded it was quite different from that which latecomers held as they re-explored the area. As Frank Craven has indicated, the twentieth-century visitor "looks out from land over water, whereas the first settlers more frequently looked from water over land. He naturally thinks of land surrounded by water, but they thought of water surrounded

15

by land. He tends to interpret the problem of settlement
in terms of acquiring control of a large area of contiguous territory; they thought of it primarily in terms of
the security of navigation" (*Southern Colonies in the
Seventeenth Century*, 1949, pp. 73-74).

The bay and the rivers and creeks that flowed into it
were significant factors in the economic and social life
of the Chesapeake Country. The enclosing peninsula—
the "Eastern Shore"—flanked a body of water two hundred miles long and forty in width at its greatest breadth.
Into the Chesapeake flowed four great rivers—the James,
the York, the Rappahannock, and the Potomac—the
first and fourth rising beyond the Blue Ridge, the second
and third on the hither side of that mountain range.
Maryland and Virginia fronted on the Chesapeake
from two directions. They shared the Potomac as a common boundary. The Shenandoah River, tributary of the
Potomac, paralleled the western side of the Blue Ridge.
Its valley served as a natural gateway from the Great
Valley of Pennsylvania, through which Germans and
Scotch-Irish reached upland Virginia and Carolina. The
"Albemarle overflow" of colonists from Virginia passed
beyond the limits of the Old Dominion, but that isolated
corner of North Carolina was in some of its economy a
part of the Chesapeake Country.

Character of the Chesapeake Country. Such was
the first occupied area that would eventually become a
part of the South. It was a region settled by Englishmen
in the seventeenth and eighteenth centuries, with German and Scotch-Irish cultures moving into Piedmont
and tramontane valley during the eighteenth to compete
with the older English civilization and to produce, as
Thomas Jefferson Wertenbaker has shown, a melting pot
that mingled the essentials of all three groups. The Chesapeake Country was an area of tobacco, grown by planters
and farmers alike; but it was also a land of Indian corn
and wheat, of hunting and fishing, of clash with Indian
tribes, of intercolonial strife, of disease and death, of
culture and illiteracy, of religious conformity and dis-
sension, of conflict with governors, kings, and Parliament. In short, it was normal in its diversity of human
as well as physical geography, in complexities that

sharply supplemented the development of social, economic, and political patterns.

The Old Dominion. The larger of the two major Chesapeake colonies, the old Dominion of Virginia, began as a joint stock company that spent some £200,000 in promoting the enterprise before it surrendered its charter in 1624 and became a royal province. Meanwhile, the London stockholders under Sir Edwin Sandys' leadership provided for a colonial legislature. In 1619 Governor George Yeardley, the councilors, and two burgesses from each of eleven districts met at Jamestown in the first representative assembly on American soil. Its first order of business was an English heritage: the membership qualifications of burgesses from two places were questioned. Representatives from one of them were denied seats. (*See Document No. 1.*) The House of Burgesses survived the surrender of the charter, and Virginians clung jealously and tenaciously to the right of participation in colonial government. Actually, the establishment of representative government was not born of protest against English tyranny, nor was it primarily an evidence of a democratic trend. Nevertheless, Virginia's elected assembly became a self-governing instrument, a training school in political democracy, and a precedent for other colonies that would become the United States.

Embryo democracy in Virginia did not run an uninterrupted course. Royal governors dissolved the assembly at will; but, emulating the House of Commons, the burgesses acquired considerable control over the purse strings, and recalcitrant executives brought them together again. Governor William Berkeley in the post-Restoration period reduced both council and burgesses to subserviency by favors such as illegal acquisitions of land. Refusing new elections, he retained in office burgesses elected when the royal cause was popular following the restoration of Charles II. Smooth sailing was interrupted in 1676 when Nathaniel Bacon, a well-educated member of the gentry newly arrived in the colony, led Virginians in revolt. An Indian uprising on the frontier, in which savages slaughtered farmers and their families, precipitated rebellion against the governor, who did nothing to protect his people. The revolt, successful at first, melted away with young Bacon's death, and Berkeley became even more tyrannical before he relinquished the governorship. Despite clashes between royal governor and colonial assembly, and periods of depression when tobacco culture was unprofitable, Virginia expanded and prospered through much of the colonial period.

Proprietary Maryland. Notwithstanding some differences in forms of government, Virginia and Maryland exhibited a minimum of divergence. The less populous colony north of the Potomac was founded as a proprietary province in 1634. Except for a few years, members of the Calvert family continued as lords proprietors until the Revolution, profiting more than any other such functionaries from quitrents—fixed annual rental fees in lieu of feudal obligations. The Catholic Lords Baltimore granted toleration to believers in Christ's divinity, but the Anglican Church became the religion of state at the turn of the century. While the proprietor was granted nearly unlimited authority, Englishmen in Maryland demanded personal liberties guaranteed by common law and a share in government through elected representatives. In the beginning the lord proprietor framed bills and sent them to the assembly for approval or rejection; but members of the colonial legislature insisted on the usual procedure in lawmaking.

Origin of Tobacco Culture. The colonies of the Chesapeake Country turned early in their history to the cultivation of tobacco. John Rolfe, future husband of Pocahontas, grew a crop of strong but sweet-scented tobacco in 1612, and soon Virginians at Jamestown had found a staple. Twenty thousand pounds were exported to England in 1619; eight years later a half million were sent to the homeland. English authorities, including James I, discouraged its production, preferring wine and silk. But the plant was adapted to soil and climate, the English market absorbed the increasing bulk for home consumption or for re-exportation, and production expanded in time to Maryland and Albemarle and in the eighteenth century to Virginia's upland. By the Revolution the Chesapeake Country was shipping annually to England a hundred million pounds of tobacco, of which four million came from North Carolina. Overproduction sometimes depressed the price, but efforts to curtail output failed to reduce it. Almost from the very beginning, tobacco became the area's great money crop, and largely conditioned its economic and social life. As Wertenbaker puts it, "The requirements of the plant determined the character of immigration, the labor system, the apportionment of land, the daily life of the planter" (*The First Americans*, 1927, p. 23).

The Labor Supply: Indentured Servants. The tobacco colonies found a partial solution to their problem of labor supply in the seventeenth century by importing indentured servants and a limited number of Africans; in the eighteenth they resorted chiefly to Negro slaves. Laborers were available in the homeland, but as the annual pay of farm hands did not exceed fifty shillings, they could not in a lifetime save sufficient money to pay the cost of transportation to the New World. Ship captains were willing to transport workers to the colonies and receive remuneration from importing planters who bought the services of their laborers for periods that averaged about four years. Englishmen—and other Europeans—whose future in their homelands held little hope of advancement, were willing to enter indenture contracts and labor for their board and keep. Not all of them willingly sold themselves into temporary service, for criminals, paupers, vagrants, and kidnapped persons were transplanted by public authority.

During the last two-thirds of the century, Virginia imported annually some 1,500 to 2,000 indentured servants, a total that ran to more than a hundred thousand by 1700. Importations to Maryland swelled annual arrivals to about 2,500. But as laborers became free after the expiration of their periods of service, the number of indentures at any time in the major tobacco colonies was about 10,000, who formed during the latter half of the century only a small percentage of the total population. A few members of graduating classes became tenants or skilled artisans; some moved to Middle Atlantic colonies; a large number became yeoman farmers who planted tobacco crops of their own, in competition with their former employers. As tobacco, unlike sugar or rice, could be cultivated profitably on a small scale, the farmer with his few acres and the labor of his own family could grow it successfully.

Plebeian and Patrician on the Potomac. Despite the development of some large plantations on either side of the Potomac, the Chesapeake Country did not become in the seventeenth century a land of large plantations worked by servants and slaves. Yeoman farmers with a few hundred acres at most were much the larger part of the population. Some of them reached the House of Burgesses, county clerkships and courts, and other positions of trust and responsibility. As a sample statistic, at least thirteen of the thirty burgesses of 1663 presumably began life in the Old Dominion as servants. Yeoman farmers also dominated Maryland agriculture, though here, as in Virginia, planter aristocracy appeared. Across the Virginia line in Albemarle, planters were few in an area inhabited mainly by backwoods plain people.

A Home-Grown Aristocracy. Historical documents such as court records and rent rolls indicate that the aristocracy of the tobacco colonies was largely home grown: that F.F.V.'s, or F.F.C.'s (First Families of the Chesapeake) had not formerly been First Families of England. Some aristocrats migrated to the colonies and occupied positions of trust; but enterprise, industry, thrift, and ability developed men who accumulated large landholdings and held important offices. The heyday of the planter aristocracy awaited the eighteenth century—and the resort to slave labor.

Origin and Development of Negro Slavery. The twenty Negroes brought to Virginia in 1619 do not mark the beginnings of slavery in the colonies. As a matter of fact, slavery as a well-defined institution did not appear until a century later. That servile status was neither imported nor imitated, and it bore no relationship to any unique qualities of the African. Rather, European practices were adjusted to conditions in the New World. There was no clear line of demarcation between servants and "slaves" as European empires dawned in America. Negroes who arrived in the early years of the Chesapeake colonies were regarded as indentured servants, some of whom completed periods of service. Their status, like that of many white servants, was indeterminate.

The institution of slavery arose in Virginia in the seventeenth century through custom, with legal recognition beginning during its second half. Early masters who purchased slaves claimed that they bought their services for life. The early court records refer to Negroes as servants, seldom as slaves. The fact that they were usually not bound for a period of years enhanced their value. An imported Negro cost about £30; a white servant, half that amount. It was only a step from the concept of a Negro as a servant for life to the concept of Negro as slave.

A series of acts passed by the Virginia colonial assembly in the second half of the seventeenth century recognized what custom was already creating. Acts regulating relations with the Indians, trade with the Dutch, and penalties for absconding servants indirectly recognized the institution. Neither these pieces of legislation nor an act of 1662—all children born in Virginia should "be bond or free only according to the condition of the mother"—created slavery. In 1680 a slave police law was passed, and from that time forward a slave code became a part of the Old Dominion's social and economic system. Virginia's neighbors—Maryland, Delaware, and North Carolina—drew heavily upon the provisions of her code; and as migrants from the "mother of colonies" participated in the westward movement, their experiences in the Old Dominion influenced legislation as far away as Texas and Missouri. Meanwhile, the basis of slavery shifted from religion to race.

Rural Life in the Chesapeake Country. Slavery gave the Chesapeake Country one of the elements that would eventually make it Southern. Ruralness was another factor that contributed to the same end. Tobacco industry and thinness of soil produced scattered homesteads and decentralized government. For convenience some planters kept shops or stores and sold to their neighbors. There were projects at various times to establish towns in Virginia, but they did not always materialize. Annapolis and Baltimore made Maryland somewhat less rural than Virginia.

Wharf Trade and Mediums of Exchange. The wharf system of trade partially compensated for lack of

towns, and at the same time hindered their development. Preparatory to shipment, tobacco hogsheads were
stored in warehouses erected at intervals of a dozen miles
on rivers and bays. By sundry inspection laws in Virginia
and Maryland, agents scrutinized tobacco and certified
to its weight and quality; and producers of the staple received "tobacco notes" or warehouse receipts. These
served as a medium of exchange in payment of taxes and
tithes. Another medium was a bill of exchange on a London bank. Tobacco was shipped to a London agent,
against whom a draft was drawn which could be used for
the liquidation of debts while the tobacco was in transit.
Neither Maryland nor Virginia developed well-defined
tradesmen until the late colonial era. English merchants
stocked warehouses with manufactured goods, and some
planters imported more commodities than they needed
for their own use. A few engaged actively in the Indian
trade. Their chief concern, however, was agriculture
rather than the market place.

Slavery Transforms the Chesapeake Area. The
eighteenth century witnessed a remarkable transforma-
tion in the social and economic life of the Old Dominion
and to a lesser extent of Maryland. The cause of the
revolution was increasing reliance on slave labor. At the
beginning of the century Virginia's Negroes numbered
6,000 as against 60,000 whites. By 1763 the number of
slaves increased to 100,000, and Maryland's to half that
number. Ambitious farmers purchased slaves, and some
of them or their descendants became well-to-do planters.
The Old Dominion, once dominated by a yeoman class,
was converted into a colony controlled by slaveholders
large and small. Some of the less fortunate farmers sought
new homes on the frontier or migrated to other colonies.

3

CAROLINA-GEORGIA LOW COUNTRY

The Carolina–Georgia Low Country, like the Chesapeake area, comprised parts of three colonies; and like its northern neighbor, it ignored provincial boundary lines in developing an economic-social regime. The old Rice Coast stretched from the Cape Fear River of North Carolina to the St. Johns River of Florida. It extended some thirty miles in depth to the pine barrens, which effectively restrained migration to the Carolina upcountry. The Low Country included the islands that skirted the sea.

The Founding of Carolina. Carolina, chartered as a single colony in 1663, was granted to eight English noblemen as a proprietary province. The lords proprietors engaged John Locke to frame the Fundamental Constitutions, but this theoretical scheme of land grants and government proved unworkable in the American wilderness. Drawing upon the social theory of the century as well as upon decadent feudalism, it contemplated an ennobled landed aristocracy with lords, proprietors, landgraves, and caciques; manor lords called "gentlemen commoners"; and yeoman farmers with landholdings of fifty acres as a voting qualification. A bicameral legislature was provided, but top-heavy administration assured the constitution's defeat by the settlers. The colony eventually conformed to the English pattern of governor and assembly and early in the eighteenth century became the two provinces of North and South Carolina. South Carolina prospered from the beginning; North Carolina enjoyed a measure of prosperity after the proprietors relinquished control.

23

Origins of North Carolina. Virginians, as we have seen, settled in the "province of Albemarle" before the Carolina charter was issued. Planters and farmers in the area became increasingly provincial because of their isolated location. Traders from Virginia, the New England colonies, and occasionally Bermuda purchased their surplus corn, tobacco, and cattle. The Cape Fear region remained largely unsettled until 1725, its upper reaches a few years longer. By the middle of the eighteenth century the colony numbered 30,000 slaves among its total population of 80,000, and by the outbreak of the Revoluton it had outdistanced its southern neighbor. Despite sizable plantations along the coast, small farms dominated the colony. Tobacco culture was important in the region of Albemarle Sound, rice cultivation south of the Cape Fear River, but staple economy was less significant in North Carolina than in Virginia–Maryland or in South Carolina–Georgia. Small farmers found the province a congenial locale, with grain and meat animals, along with naval stores, yielding slow advancement. (*See Document No. 2.*)

Settlement of South Carolina. The permanent "Charles Town" was settled on Charleston Harbor in 1680 by Barbadians and by Englishmen direct from the homeland. Settlers from Scotland, Ireland, and Wales, from German states and Switzerland, and from New England colonies augmented the population. French Huguenots, many of them skilled laborers, established themselves not only in Charleston but also up the Cooper and Santee rivers. Farming, lumbering, and Indian trade gave early inhabitants means of subsistence. Eventually rice and indigo acquired major economic status. By the end of the eighteenth century's first quarter some 14,000 whites and 32,000 slaves inhabited the colony.

Georgia: A Trusteeship. Three motives prompted Englishmen in the founding of Georgia. An imperialistic policy designed it as a buffer colony on the Indian-Spanish frontier. The mercantilistic theory of national wealth prompted a province that would yield raw products not grown in England or in other colonies. The unemployment problem in London and in other cities might be solved by a colony that welcomed ne'er-do-wells, even though they had been jailed for their pauperism.

In 1729 James Edward Oglethorpe was made chairman of a committee of Parliament to investigate debtor prisons. The investigation resulted in the release of many thousands of prisoners whose lot was not improved by freedom. A group of "Thomas Bray Associates," promoters of social betterment, petitioned George 1 for a grant of land as a haven for economic and social relief. Georgia thus became, in 1732, a trusteeship—a colony to be held in trust by trustees who were not to profit from the enterprise, in land grants or otherwise. The trustees raised money by subscription to pay the expenses of insolvent but honest migrants to Georgia and to subsist them there for at least a year. The regime in its early years was paternalistic, with prohibitions aplenty: no speculation in land, no mortgages, no slaves, no rum, for these things might prevent rehabilitation. Experts in silk culture and wine pressing were sent over. Each settler who migrated at the expense of the trusteeship was given fifty acres of land. Five hundred was a maximum for those who came at their own expense. Land was held in tale male to develop a fighting frontier in a frontier province.

Five thousand settlers removed to the colony by 1737. Six years later the population was 500, for most of the migrants scattered to the four winds. Prohibition of slavery and rum made Georgia seem an uninviting place. The trustees ran amuck financially, the charter was surrendered to the crown in 1751, and Georgia became, in the quarter century before the Revolution, a normal Southern agricultural community. Shortly before the end of the colonial period its population was estimated at 18,000 whites and 15,000 Negroes.

Rice Culture. "Seed from Madagascar" marked the beginning of rice culture near the end of the seventeenth century, an industry that reached large proportions a generation later. Originating in the Charleston neighborhood, it expanded northward to the Cape Fear River of North Carolina and southward along the Georgia coast after removal of the Spanish menace through the transfer of the Floridas from Spain to England.

Inland cypress swamps, flooded from reservoirs filled by rains, springs, and streams, served the rice plant for most of the century. Toward its end, however, the tide-flow system of inundation largely supplanted the use of reservoirs. The ebb and flow of the tide in rivers that traversed the Rice Coast provided a supply of water that flooded fields at high tide through sluice gates in embankments and permitted drainage at low tide by reversing the process of opening and closing them. Seed rice was planted in spring months on ground prepared the previous fall. Sprout flow, point flow, long flow, lay-by flow, were stages in rice culture, with cultivation following the second and third. Reaping with sickles began early in September. This antiquated tool continued in general use until the Civil War, though a few planters employed scythes with cradles. After drying in the field, rice was bundled and carried to barn or stack either by slaves atop their heads or by "flats" that floated on the field's canal. Threshing was done sometimes by treading but usually with the flail; the separation of husk from seed required a mortar and fat pine pestle. Winnowing and screening completed the process, except for barreling the grain for market.

South Carolinians found a profitable market for their rice crop in Portugal, where it soon acquired a monopoly, and they exported some to the foreign West Indies. Such shipments brought conflict with the homeland, whose navigation laws forbade the trade. The strife was eased in 1730 when Parliament provided that rice could be carried direct from South Carolina to European ports south of Cape Finisterre. The benefits of this arrangement were soon extended to North Carolina and then to Georgia. By the beginning of the Revolution the colonies of North and South Carolina and Georgia were exporting about 165,000 barrels.

Slave Labor on the Rice Coast. The Rice Coast's economy before the introduction of the staple was not conducive to the use of slave labor on a large scale. The production of rice encouraged the importation of Negroes, and they soon became a numerous part of the population. Producers were convinced that whites could not endure the unhealthy working conditions in malaria-infested swamps. They therefore resorted to slave labor to clear the land, dig the ditches, cultivate the crop, and harvest it for market. Even among Negroes the mortality rate was high in the colonial era. The average slaveholding was larger than in the Chesapeake Country; and farmers with few slaves or none were a smaller portion of the white population.

South Carolina's slave code, like Virginia's, evolved from specific enactments to meet problems as they arose to comprehensive laws that summarized past experiences. A general act of 1712 incorporated many provisions of a Barbadian law of a quarter century before, and a serious slave revolt a generation later resulted in supplementary regulations. Basic in control measures were those that restricted slave mobility and assemblage, prohibited possession of arms and consumption of liquor, and forbade the teaching of slaves to read and write. Legislation also provided punishment for crimes and misdemeanors and inferior courts to try cases involving slaves. The South Carolina code served as a model for Georgia; Florida found the Georgia code useful in enacting laws in the 1820's; and other states were directly or indirectly influenced by the South Carolina pattern.

Eliza Lucas and the Introduction of Indigo Culture. Indigo became a secondary staple crop in the South Carolina–Georgia Lowlands about the middle of the eighteenth century. Teen-age Eliza Lucas, daughter of the governor of Antigua, began experimenting with the plant in 1741, and within a few years she not only grew it successfully but also learned the method of converting the plant into dye. Seeds were distributed to other planters, who found the crop a valuable supplement to rice, for the two crops could be grown with the same labor supply. To encourage production, Parliament provided a bounty of sixpence per pound in 1748, and England served as a ready market for the product. By the end of the colonial period 20,000 acres yielded an annual crop of over a million pounds. The Revolution stopped the bounty and closed the market. Efforts to revive cultivation after 1783 resulted largely in failure. But the South Carolina–Georgia Lowlands soon discovered another product, sea-island cotton, to take its place in their economy.

Meanwhile Eliza Lucas had married a prominent South Carolinian, Charles Pinckney, and given birth to two sons, Charles Cotesworth and Thomas, who made notable contributions in establishing the new Republic.

Charleston as an Economic Focus. In contrast with the Chesapeake Country, with rivers that admitted ocean-going vessels and a wharf system of trade that discouraged development of towns, South Carolina emerged as a city state. To a lesser extent Savannah served the Georgia Coast, though Charleston supplemented Savannah as a commercial focus for the colony across the river. Beaufort and Georgetown also became local centers of trade, but Charleston became the great emporium. Sea islands skirting the coast provided an inland waterway that served as a highway for small craft, and numerous inlets, streams, and rivers penetrated the interior. Good roads, with bridges and ferries to cross streams, impressed travelers. Rice and indigo, produce from the interior, and deerskins from the Indian trade found their way to the South Carolina city, where factors served as agents for London merchants. Ships that departed laden with products of the land returned with English merchandise required by free and slave population.

South Carolina's prosperity had a relatively broad base. In 1718 it exported nearly ten thousand barrels of rice, but it also shipped beef and pork, corn and peas, leather and hides, furs and deerskins, pitch and tar. Its importations included flour and salt fish from Northern colonies; sugar, molasses, rum, and slaves from the West Indies; wines from the Madeira Islands and Mediterranean ports; and manufactured goods from the homeland. The shops of Charleston's local merchants handled home-grown produce; and after the middle of the eighteenth century, pork, wheat, and flour from the back country were exchanged there for manufactured items. Artisans' shops thrived in the colonial capital.

Charleston as a Political and Social Capital. Charleston was not only the commercial focus; it was also the political capital of the colony. Until 1719 it was the sole polling place in the province; and until 1769 all governmental activity centered there. Even after a measure of local justice was provided in that year, the Court of Common Pleas still had a large share in administering justice for the whole colony. Charleston remained the focal point for political activity. There the governor resided, there the assembly sat, and there Indian affairs were administered. Wealthy planters of the Rice Coast, who employed overseers more extensively than tobacco growers, abandoned their plantations from May until the middle of autumn to escape malaria and to enjoy Charleston society. Their town houses were often occupied in the winter, too, for Charleston society offered balls and races and clubs as well as routine fraternizing that contrasted with the occasional visitors and parties in rural areas.

Charleston was the only city of any size south of Philadelphia, and yet it reached only modest proportions in the colonial period. By 1790 its population stood at 15,000, divided about equally between free and slave. Nevertheless, it "was then perhaps the most urbane of American cities, with a notable semipublic library, thriving bookstores, excellent newspapers, mantua makers and milliners, in touch with Paris fashions, a thronged race course, dancing assemblies, and easy-mannered men's clubs" (Ulrich B. Phillips, *Life and Labor in the Old South,* 1929, p. 52). Its eighteenth-century atmosphere survived into the twentieth, with a residential area rather than wharves at the peninsula's point, with the ends of three-story houses rather than their fronts abutting the streets, and with a skyline of trees rather than of towering buildings.

South Carolina Separateness. The Carolina-Georgia Low Country, unlike the early tobacco area, permitted no extension of its staple economy to the westward. It was a compact community that reached its natural limits by the middle of the eighteenth century. The plantation regime dominated the agricultural scene more completely than in the Chesapeake Tidewater of tobacco. Prospering through its commercial connections with the homeland and the West Indies, South Carolina "developed a sense of separateness" augmented by limited contacts with other commonwealths to the north. In the years that lay ahead, it would assert its rights with much vehemence, and South Carolinians would venerate the state more than other Americans. Nationality, whether American or Southern, would be strenuously resisted among a people who accepted a concept of particularism.

— 4 —

WESTWARD EXPANSION

Upcountry and Valley Frontier. The South in its pioneer years, like other American areas from the Atlantic to the Pacific, was affected by the process known as frontier. The first southern "West," as Frederick Jackson Turner pointed out many years ago, was the Tidewater region from Maryland south to Georgia. "Frontiersmen" arrived earliest in the Chesapeake Coastal Plain, later in Carolina, and eventually in Georgia. But long before the last received settlers, even before the first and second became well established, hardy pioneers had explored the Back Country, a region that Turner designated the Old West. Paradoxically, the westward movement was not always in a westerly direction. Except for Virginia's Piedmont north of the James, upcountry settlers came by the thousands from the Great Valley of Pennsylvania, through the Shenandoah Valley of Virginia and watergaps in the Blue Ridge, in search of land in southern Virginia and the Carolinas. The pine barrens between the Low Country and the fall line were for years an effective barrier to westward migration.

The Piedmont Plateau contained much rolling land,

with rugged hills as it approached the mountains. It was not an unbroken area of forest, for in addition to natural meadows, Indians had burned large patches. It was "a rare combination of woodland and pasture, with clear running streams and mild climate." Heavy rainfall made erosion a problem after land was cleared. Much of the soil was rich, and farms yielded adequate livings. Its streams provided transportation as far as the fall line, where rapids required wagon hauling to the lower reaches of the rivers.

Germans and Ulster Scots in Piedmont and Valley. Soon after Englishmen and a few indentures and slaves crossed Virginia's fall line into the Piedmont, two other streams of homeseekers reached the new frontier from Pennsylvania. These were the Germans and Scotch-Irish. Both found America an inviting environment. Protestants from sundry German states, notably the Palatinate, poured into Pennsylvania's Great Valley at the rate of 1,500 a year beginning with the great exodus of 1717. Many of them or their descendants moved southward into western Maryland and the Shenandoah Valley, and then, as we have seen, eastward through watergaps in the Blue Ridge to the Piedmont. Although the Palatine Germans "were pacific, law-abiding, stolid, deeply pious, temperate, and devoted to the social ideal of a well-ordered society," Carl Bridenbaugh says, they were also "shrewd and calculating and determined to achieve worldly prosperity as well as spiritual joys to a degree that led those who knew them not to accuse them of materialism."

Simultaneously, the Ulster Scots sought land and freedom across the Atlantic. English encroachments on their rights in Ulster made them "emotional, courageous, aggressive, pugnacious, fiercely intolerant." They were "hard-drinking, with a tendency to indolence," but "they nevertheless produced ambitious leaders with the virtues of the warrior and politician" (*Myths and Realities,* 1952, p. 133). Like the Germans, many passed into the Shenandoah Valley, where some found permanent abodes. The valley and watergaps served as a natural gateway for those who sought homes in the Piedmont. (*See Document No. 3.*)

Frontier Life and Labor. Migrants to the new frontier, whether Germans, Ulsterites, Highland Scots, Welsh, Swiss, or English Quakers, were for the most part "humble folk," though a few who owned slaves and many acres lived on the uplands or in the valley. The log cabin, gift of the Swedes from forested Scandinavia, was the typical frontier steading, whether in the Piedmont or farther west beyond the mountains. With the help of neighbors, some of whom might live miles away, a cabin of round logs might be erected in a day. A dwelling of square-hewn logs, prevalent among the Germans, was a more time-consuming structure, and so was the "Palatine Barn" with stone basement, threshing floor, and haymow. The Germans introduced the covered Conestoga wagon as a travel conveyance from Pennsylvania to their ultimate destination, and also as a vehicle for transporting surplus crops to nearby markets.

In addition to horses or oxen, a cow and some poultry, the frontiersman's essential equipment included axe and rifle. With the axe he built a cabin, cleared ten or fifteen acres of land—often a community enterprise known as log-rolling—and shaped farm tools, dishes, and furniture. With the rifle he brought down game, held Indians at bay, and dispatched outlaws. Frontier life was a family affair, with half-grown boys handling the long rifle and the crude plow, and the womenfolk using spinning wheel and loom for domestic manufacture of clothing to supplement that made from deerskins. Frontiersmen lived primitive, individualistic, self-sufficient lives as they converted nature's bounty to human existence.

Frontier Leadership. Among the pioneers who settled in Valley and Piedmont in pre-Revolutionary years were several conspicuous leaders and forebears of others. Especially significant were Daniel Boone, James Robertson, and John Sevier. Their contemporaries included the ancestors of other notable Americans: Calhoun and Polk, Crockett and Houston, Lincoln and Jefferson Davis and Stonewall Jackson. Jefferson lived at the edge of the Blue Ridge, and Andrew Jackson's father migrated from the coast to the Carolina Piedmont a few years before the Revolution.

Seaboard and Back Country Antagonisms. The establishment of a new Back Country society produced antagonisms with the older established communities along the seaboard. In North and South Carolina in particular, conflicts reached critical proportions on the eve of the Revolution. Overrepresentation of the low counties in the colonial assembly, high taxes, corrupt officials, and inefficient administration of justice led to protests and then open rebellion to secure a redress of grievances. In North Carolina resistance began in the late 1750's, but the Regulator movement did not materialize for another decade. Protesting farmers united to resist inequitable taxation and greedy officials. The Regulators sought peaceful redress of their grievances until Governor William Tryon proclaimed them insurrectionists. When protestants broke up the Hillsboro supreme court and maltreated lawyers and officials, including Edmund Fanning, register of Orange County, Tryon led the militia against the Regulators and defeated them at the battle of the Alamance in 1771. Some of the Regulator leaders were executed, some others left North Carolina.

The Regulator movement in South Carolina sprang from the same causes, but upcountry South Carolinians suffered from another abuse: there were no courts in the Back Country, infested with lawbreakers. Honest farmers took justice into their own hands and served notice on the malefactors that they should reform or quit the colony. Desultory fighting between Regulars and militia stopped short of civil war when the legislature was summoned to provide local justice in 1769. The act provided only a partial measure of redress, for while it established a system of circuit courts, with a sheriff for each district, only the evidence was heard in the locality. Legal processes still originated in the Court of Common Pleas at Charleston, and the evidence was returnable there for decision. Upcountry counties were unrepresented in the legislature before the Revolution; thereafter they had fewer delegates than their population warranted.

Beginnings of the Old Southwest. The end of the French and Indian War in 1763 opened a vast territory, formerly claimed by France, to English and American

settlement. Despite King George III's proclamation of
that year, forbidding settlement west of the Appalachian
divide until his agents negotiated treaties with the Indians peacefully dispossessing them of their lands, empire policy did not necessarily mean a permanent barrier
to westward expansion. Land speculators, British and
American, were ready to exploit the tramontane area as
they had earlier the seaboard or the upcountry. Not
long after Pontiac's defeat, Indian agents negotiated
the treaty of Fort Stanwix with the Iroquois (1768) by
which they surrendered to the crown a vast area between the headwaters of the Ohio and Tennessee rivers.

Vandalia—Westsylvania—West Virginia. A syndi-
cate of English and American speculators sought a
grant of land in the ceded territory with the view of
planting Vandalia colony in present-day West Virginia,
but with overlapping into southwestern Pennsylvania
and eastern Kentucky. The Privy Council approved the
project for a "fourteenth colony," and the patent was
ready for the king's signature when the Revolution began in the spring of 1775. A few bold pioneers inhabited
the area as early as the middle of the eighteenth century.
While some abandoned the region during the French
and Indian War, enough were there to demand statehood by the Revolution. Soon after the Declaration of
Independence, inhabitants sent a memorial to Congress
depicting the state of confusion, the Indian problem, and
their natural rights to the lands upon which they had
settled. They petitioned Congress for recognition as the
State of Westsylvania. Virginia members objected, and
Congress declined recognition. The movement for statehood was not abandoned; and eventually, in 1863, West
Virginia was admitted to the Union.

Watauga Association—State of Franklin—Tennessee. After the failure of the North Carolina Regula-
tion's initial phase, a few of the Regulators removed to
the Watauga and Holston rivers in present-day East Tennessee. They were soon joined by James Robertson and
some of his Yadkin River neighbors from western North
Carolina. Marylanders and Virginians, too, crossed the
mountains by way of Cumberland Gap, some of them
settling unknowingly south of the Virginia line. Among

the Shenandoah Valley migrants was John Sevier, son of a French Huguenot, destined as was Robertson to become a state-maker in founding Tennessee. North Carolina could give no protection against outlaws and Indians, nor could its government secure titles to land grants. Settlers on the headwaters of the Tennessee drew up the Articles of the Watauga Association in 1772, a squatters' agreement that provided a governing body of five commissioners to raise a militia, record land titles, issue marriage licenses, and try offenders. Among exploits of its leaders, Robertson led a group of settlers to the Cumberland who became the founders of Nashborough and Middle Tennessee. And soon thereafter John Sevier escorted 240 men across the Great Smokies to participate in the victory at King's Mountain. After the Revolution Wataugans became increasingly dissatisfied with the failure of North Carolina's government to serve them effectively, and a movement for separate statehood began. Delegates met at Jonesboro to set up the State of Franklin, with "Nolichucky Jack" Sevier as governor. The movement led a precarious existence until 1788, when Franklin became a part of Tennessee. The state was admitted to the Union in 1796 with Sevier as governor.

Transylvania-Kentucky. The frontier hero responsible for opening up the "Dark and Bloody Ground" of Kentucky to settlement was Daniel Boone, fortunate in his ghostwriter, John Filson, who surrounded him with myth as well as merit. In the late 1760's he left his home on the Yadkin to hunt with a small party of men beyond Cumberland Gap. After a year and a half roaming the beautiful land, he spread glowing reports of his western paradise among his neighbors and led a small band of them to make a permanent home. Meanwhile James Harrod and George Rogers Clark and other Pennsylvanians and Virginians made a settlement at Harrodsburg. It was Richard Henderson, however, who made the first organized effort to found a new commonwealth. Aristocrat rather than backwoodsman, he formed a partnership of land speculators, the Transylvania Company, which bought the land between the Cumberland, Kentucky, and Ohio rivers from the Cherokee Indians.

Boone and "thirty guns" were selected to cut a Wilderness Road to the Kentucky River.

Courageous, bold, self-reliant, and venturesome, Boone was an excellent choice to serve as a vanguard for the proposed settlement. In the spring of 1775 he founded Boonesborough. Meanwhile, other pioneers had built their cabins, and Henderson called a convention of delegates from four settlements, to whom he read a constitution. The proprietors petitioned Congress for recognition as a fourteenth state. The people of Harrodsburg, however, sent a petition to the Virginia legislature asking that commonwealth to extend its authority over Kentucky. As a result, much of present-day Kentucky became a county of the Old Dominion, and the Transylvania project came to an end. Kentucky became a state in 1792.

Grievances of Pioneers in the Old Southwest. Thus no one of the projects to establish a fourteenth colony before the Revolution, or a fourteenth state during the war, materialized. But the attempts illustrate Western problems and grievances against the East very much as the Carolina Regulator movements had done a short time before. Conflicting boundaries and questionable land titles, inefficient administration of justice and defense, the difficulty as well as the dislike of paying taxes, and incompatible interests between the East and the West were reasons why residents demanded independent statehood.

Economic Potential of the Old Southwest. The Old Southwest was chiefly Western in the Revolutionary period. Parts of it would become, in future years, Southern in institutions and ideas. A land of rich soil, inhabited by elk and deer and buffalo and wild turkeys as well as Indians, the tramontane region continued to attract settlers who came by way of the Gap and the Wilderness Road, or descended the Ohio in canoes and other craft. Pioneers depleted the supply of wild game, but cattle and hogs and sheep provided a substitute for subsistence as well as for export; and horses, faster than their line-aged Virginia forebears, made racing the sport of Bluegrass parvenus. Saline springs gave a bountiful supply of salt for man and beast, and bourbon an ever-flowing quencher of thirst, albeit mint juleps never attained the stature they reached in Old Virginia. Tobacco culture, too, crossed the mountains to Bluegrass and Pennyroyal, and hemp became a valuable subsidiary.

The Indian Frontier. Long before Boone and Henderson and Robertson and Sevier crossed the mountains to pioneer in backwoods and Bluegrass, Anglo-Americans met redskins and Latins on an ever-receding frontier. The first arrivals in the Chesapeake Country discovered that Indians were both a means and a menace. They provided the ubiquitous John Smith with grain to relieve the "Starving Time"; and the marriage of John Rolfe to Powhatan's daughter Pocahontas augmented peaceful relations between reds and whites. But in 1622 that chief's successor, in a different frame of mind, took the warpath and massacred 357 Virginians. Survivors retaliated with forays and foragings, and peace followed for a score of years. While Indian raids were seldom as formidable as this one, experiences of peace and war and peace again were repeated time after time.

Fortunately for the white man, trading with the Indians was fully as important as warring with them. From Maryland south to Georgia, Anglo-Americans plied a trade in deer and buffalo and bearskins in the seventeenth and eighteenth centuries. In return the transgressors supplied beads and blankets, knives and hatchets, tomahawks and guns, powder and lead, clothing and rum. The effectiveness of white men's "firewater," their propensity to cheat naïve natives, and the red men's failure to comprehend the meaning of "agreements" whereby they surrendered lands in perpetuity to their white neighbors alienated many of them.

The Indian Problem in International Rivalry. The Southern Indian problem was complicated by the existence of other colonial enterprises on the periphery of the Anglo-American South. Spaniards in the Floridas and the French in Louisiana were also vying not only for the Indian trade but also for allies in competition for empire. The conflict involved the frontier south of Virginia, for Carolina and then Georgia were chartered to

expand it toward Spanish and French territory. From
small beginnings toward the end of the seventeenth century, Carolinians became aggressive in the early part of
the eighteenth. The problem was simplified by treaties
that ended the French and Indian War, for France was
eliminated from the Mississippi Valley and the Floridas
became English territory at the same time.

Four nations of Southern Indians were significantly
involved in the commercial and international complexities before the Spanish and French menaces were removed in 1763. The Cherokee confederacy inhabited
western parts of both Carolinas, eastern Tennessee, and
northern Georgia and Alabama. Members abandoned
their Anglo-American allies in 1760, and suffered chas-
tisement as a result. The Creeks occupied northern
Florida and the major portions of Georgia and Alabama.
Neutrality in the tripartite struggle left them strong but
dependent in the future upon the English for supplies.
More numerous were the Choctaw who lived in Mississippi and adjacent Alabama, fronting Louisiana and
West Florida, and strongly attached to the French. Their
neighbors to the north were the Chickasaw in northern
Mississippi and western Tennessee, pro-British and in-
veterate enemies of the French. A fifth nation, the
Catawbas, now greatly reduced in numbers, occupied a
small area in northwestern South Carolina and were firm
allies of the Carolina colonists.

Indian Traders. If Indian nations warred among
themselves and against their white neighbors, their relations with traders were usually amicable, though
fraudulent treatment by irresponsible agents aroused
their ire. Resident tradesmen in each of the towns were
generally accepted as a normal part of village life. Coun-
selors to chiefs in the realms of statecraft and defense,
they lived in affluence, sired half-breed children by
squaws who kept their houses, and acquiesced in tribal
membership of their progeny. From their ways and
works, and those of itinerant traders, Indians learned
and adopted some of the customs of white men and became more and more dependent upon commercial relations. But not entirely. Land-hungry migrants sought
their acres, demanded their removal to the trans-Mis-

sissippi West in the next century, and eventually made them wards of the nation. Meanwhile, British and Americans sought their aid in Revolutionary days.

— 5 —

THE REVOLUTIONARY GENERATION IN THE SOUTH

The quarter century between the Peace of Paris in 1763 and Washington's inauguration was more than a period of causes, course, and consequences of the American Revolution. Normal living was interrupted during the shooting war of 1775-1781, but the period as a whole was one of rapid growth in population and of economic and social advancement. The Southern provinces, which did not feel the full effect of fighting until the war was half over, contributed human and economic resources throughout the period. Before inventorying these contributions to clash and conflict, a survey of some aspects of Southern life on the eve of the Revolution may serve as an appropriate transition.

Population in 1763 and 1790. At the beginning of the period some 700,000 whites and Negroes occupied the provinces south of Mason and Dixon's line. The 275,000 slaves were distributed 100,000 to Virginia, 70,000 to South Carolina, about 50,000 to each of Maryland and North Carolina, and 5,000 to Georgia.

The white people of the South were overwhelmingly British, for Scotch-Irish, Scots, and Welsh augmented basic English stock. Of Continental Europeans, Germans, French Protestants, and Swiss contributed to numbers and cultural differences as well. Further immigration and a high birth rate resulted in rapid growth during the Revolutionary generation. Despite excessive infant mortality, large families among both whites and slaves hastened increase. Importations of Negroes from Africa and the West Indies slackened perceptibly during the war years. Departing Tories took their slaves with them, and evacuating British carried away chattel property. By the census of 1790 slave population numbered 650,000. Meanwhile, the number of whites, with faster acceleration, reached 1,200,000.

Southern Education. Education in the Southern colonies was a restricted enterprise: a private rather than a public concern. Rich planters, and a few not so wealthy, employed tutors for their children or joined with nearby patricians in engaging a teacher. Princeton graduate Philip Fithian, oft-cited because he kept a delightful journal, tutored seven children and a nephew of Robert Carter of Nomini Hall, teaching one of the sons Sallust, the youngest daughter her alphabet, and a wide range of subjects, including mathematics, English, the history of England, and classical languages, to sundry offspring. (*See Document No. 4.*) The education of planters' sons transcended formal book learning to include dancing, riding, and a practical knowledge of plantation management. Except in the fine arts and in music, education for girls seldom continued beyond elementary branches.

A few families sent their children across the Atlantic to British or Continental schools. As a medley of miscellany, Charles and John Carroll of Maryland attended Jesuit schools in France. Arthur and Richard Henry Lee, Virginians, studied at British schools, and so did Thomas Nelson, Jr., destined to become war governor of the Old Dominion; but John Laurens of South Carolina attended a Geneva private school. James Madison profited immensely from his years at Princeton. Of the nine colleges in the thirteen colonies, only William and Mary was Southern, and its clientele was largely Virginian. Three signers of the Declaration, including Jefferson, graduated there. Among the better-known academies were the grammar school maintained by William and Mary, the Presbyterian Hampden-Sydney and Liberty Hall in western parts of Virginia, and King William's (St. John's College today) at Annapolis.

Education was often a responsibility of clergymen, whether in academies or in private instruction. Lawyers, too, served the cause of education, for aspiring legalists read law in their offices. Jefferson devoted several years to the task with the learned George Wythe. The London Inns of Court attracted a limited number of young Americans, two-thirds of whom prior to 1860 came from Southern commonwealths. Among colonial South Carolinians educated there were Thomas and Charles Cotesworth Pinckney and the two Rutledges, Edward and John.

Southern Libraries. Libraries in the Southern colonies were—like education—individual concerns. Several planters in the Chesapeake area and Carolina Low Countries accumulated a few hundred volumes, though some of the collections were considerably larger. The second William Byrd's library of nearly four thousand volumes was the only one in the South that approximated Cotton Mather's in New England. Educated gentlemen assembled works on science, medicine, practical agriculture, the classics, and pious literature. At the other extreme, among the commoners, a copy of the prayer book, the Bible, and *Pilgrim's Progress* were often the only literary possessions. One public library merits mention: the Charleston Library Society's holdings numbered over six thousand volumes.

Southern Newspapers. The few newspapers in Southern colonies on the eve of conflict were products of the eighteenth century's second and third quarters. Their circulation may have reached fifteen hundred, but subscriptions by public houses gave a far larger number of readers. Local "literary" contributions, whether poetry and prose, were often of doubtful quality. Foreign news was belated: in the *South-Carolina Gazette*'s issue of September 24, 1772, the most recent European item bore the date July 14, and that newspaper sometimes awaited the arrival of a ship before going to press. The Rice Coast was served by two other Charleston papers and one published in Savannah. These and Baltimore's two *Gazettes,* Williamsburg's three, and Norfolk's one enlightened their readers on domestic as well as foreign events. Colonial papers gave increasing attention to political views as resistance to English authority reached critical proportions.

The Theater in the Colonial South.   The earliest theater anywhere in colonial America was probably William Levingston's, built at Williamsburg in 1716. By the middle of the century, appreciative audiences at Annapolis, and at smaller communities in the Chesapeake Country, could enjoy competent acting. A notable achievement occurred in 1752 when the Hallam Company opened at Williamsburg with a superior performance of *The Merchant of Venice.* Charleston's theater surpassed all others in the Southern colonies. From the 1730's until the Revolution, a succession of "New Theatres" provided good entertainment for ardent playgoers. In the winter of 1763-1764, David Douglass's British "American Company of Commedians" played every other week night before crowded houses, the receipts averaging about £100 sterling each performance. A decade later the same company staged seventy-seven operas, plays, and farces in a season unequaled in the colonial era. Charleston's St. Cecilia Society paid its chief musical performers, advertising for talent as far distant as Boston.

Recreation.   Social diversions were pursued enthusiastically by rich, yeomen, and poor alike. Planters kept a stable of horses, for racing and for riding, with fox-hunting a popular sport. Gay parties at plantation houses provided dancing for young and old; the Virginia reel and the minuet were favorite expressions of the terpsichorean art. Delectable dinners were served in grand style by servants in livery. Lesser folk also rode and hunted and raced, and threw in shooting matches and wrestling for good measure. Fairs, harvest frolics, court days, and militia musters brought people of all classes together. Religion had its recreational advantage, for the

church often served as a social institution. Many Anglican clergymen did not take their parish duties seriously;
and the Great Awakening indicated the spiritual starva-
tion of neglected people. The dissenters—Presbyterians,
Baptists, and sundry others—popularized their faiths,
particularly in the upcountry. Denominational bicker-
ings were a normal part of religious activity. (*See Document No. 3.*)

Government and Politics. Governors, whether appointed by the crown or by a proprietor, as in Maryland, reflected the interests of England and the Empire;
the assemblies, reflecting the concerns of the colonials,
became sounding boards of popular sentiment. Conflicting interests were occasionally compromised, as in the
Carolina Regulator movements. The county system of
local government prevailed, with parish vestries sometimes sharing the responsibilities of administration. In
Virginia the governor appointed justices of the peace,
who collectively formed the county court and supervised roads, issued land certificates, and apportioned
local taxes. The sheriff collected revenue at a ten per
cent fee and administered the court's findings. Gentlemen freeholders monopolized membership in county
courts as well as in the council, appointed by the king
upon recommendation of the governor. Councilors ad-
vised the executive, served as the legislature's upper
chamber, and performed judicially as a supreme court.

One Southern political order deserves notice. By the
close of the Revolutionary generation in Virginia, thirty-
five or forty thousand adult males were qualified voters,
and nearly half of them actually exercised the right of
suffrage—but only in the choice of burgesses. Appoin-
tive positions and membership in the House of Burgesses
were the pathway to power that produced such able leaders as Washington and Jefferson, Madison and Mason,
Marshall and Monroe. Did random choice bring these
Virginians to the top, or did the interplay of aristocratic
and democratic forces produce the happy result? The
two factors were neither contradictory nor mutually exclusive. The gentry provided candidates and guidance
in choosing among them; lesser freeholders determined
what gentlemen should be chosen. Plural as well as oral

voting benefited the gentry; so also did treating—"swilling the planters with bumbo." The practice, decried by some freeholders, was used effectively by such revered gentlemen as Washington, Jefferson, and Marshall. In seeking election as a burgess in 1758, Washington provided, *in absentia*, 160 gallons of assorted liquors for 391 voters and sundry "hangers-on." Fifty gallons of rum punch, twenty-eight of rum, forty-six of beer, thirty-four of wine, and two of cider royal enspirited the average consumer by a quart and a half. Washington was elected (Charles S. Sydnor, *Gentlemen Freeholders*, 1952, pp. 53, 54).

The South in the Revolution. The historian who writes of a section's participation in a great national movement such as the American Revolution must be cautious in pointing to its contributions lest he leave the impression that the men and events of which he writes played the dominant role. Washington and Jefferson were indeed Southerners, but they were acting and speaking not only as Virginians but also as Americans. Patrick Henry expressed dynamics of protest just as acceptable among New England radicals as they were among Southern revolutionary spirits, though he and George Mason were ever affected by localism. Mason's Virginia Bill of Rights and Jefferson's Statute of Virginia for Religious Freedom were significant documents that emanated from the Revolutionary generation. (*See Documents Nos. 5 and 6.*) A review of the South in the Revolution, even out of context, may serve a useful purpose in indicating how Southern men and events contributed toward a common purpose.

Grievances in the Southern Commonwealths. The causes that motivated South Atlantic folk in the growing rift with the homeland approximated those of New England and the Middle Atlantic colonies, though Southern provinces fitted better into the scheme of empire than the Northeast. Their great staples—tobacco, rice, indigo, naval stores—were welcome in England, and there was little rivalry in manufactures. Chesapeake tobacco had a near monopoly in the English market, and the production of indigo, naval stores, and pig iron was encouraged by generous bounties. Nevertheless, the mercantile system provided an avenue of complaint. Americans could ship rice and tobacco more cheaply in Dutch vessels. Commissions, insurance, and high freight rates convinced planters that profits were reduced by an inequitable system. Some were in chronic debt to their factors; and entails that prevented foreclosures often passed debts from one generation to another. On the eve of conflict planters in the Southern colonies owed English merchants some £2,000,000 notwithstanding an excess of exports over imports by something like £90,000. English merchants looked askance at colonial importation of foreign coin or bullion or the issuing of paper money.

The crown's policy of restricting settlement beyond the Proclamation Line of 1763 was a significant grievance. Such imperialism antagonized planters whose speculative interests continued into the Revolutionary era, and it also antagonized common men with the westward urge, for they, too, wanted a free field to accumulate land. Other examples of protest were Patrick Henry's resolutions against the Stamp Act in the Virginia House of Burgesses and Jefferson's *Summary View of the Rights of British America.* The interminable quarrels between English and colonial authority over the power to tax were extended to include colonial denial of Parliament's right to legislate. Until the crisis of 1774-1775, Southern colonists, like their Northern contemporaries, sought equality of rights with the homeland rather than independence. Many would have returned readily to the happier relationship of 1763.

Preliminaries of the Revolution.   Men from Southern colonies were as conscious as others of real and fancied wrongs, and fully as vocative in their protests. The furor over the passage of the Stamp Act was vigorous south of Mason and Dixon's line. Virginia, North Carolina, and Georgia sent no delegates to the Stamp Act Congress, but opposition was as pronounced in them as in Maryland and South Carolina. Sympathy for Boston was manifest in the South Atlantic colonies, some of whom sent economic aid to the beleaguered Bay Colony. The clash at Lexington and Concord excited Southern men who would soon participate in a shooting war.

Loyalists and Patriots. Not all inhabitants of the Southern colonies sided with the Patriot cause. The dramatic events leading up to the overt act of war left many undecided. The Loyalist cause was strongest in the Carolinas and Georgia, weakest in Maryland and Virginia. Lord Fairfax and William Byrd III took the king's side in the Old Dominion, Daniel Dulany in Maryland. Only Georgia experienced the return of a royal governor during the war. The leadership of the Patriot cause was chiefly aristocratic, and with the aristocracy went a majority of the common men.

The Declaration of Independence. Steps leading to the Declaration of Independence were shared by Southern commonwealths. On April 12, 1776, the North Carolina assembly voted to instruct its delegates in Congress to concur with other representatives in declaring independence. A month later a Virginia convention declared that colony independent of Britain. And on June 7 Richard Henry Lee of Virginia offered three resolutions in Congress: that the thirteen colonies were and ought to be independent, that foreign alliances should be made, and that steps should be taken to form a plan of confederation. A few days later Jefferson was made chairman of a committee to draft a declaration of independence. His famous manifesto served as a platform for the Patriot party. In its brief philosophic pronouncement, the Virginian endeavored to summarize the political thought of the century. The consent-of-the-governed theory was readily acceptable in the South; but the "self-evident truths" that all men were created equal and endowed with the inalienable rights of life, liberty, and the pursuit of happiness gave rise to much speculative thought in the years to come. His "free and equal" assertion was probably acceptable to slaveholders on the theory that only white men were involved in the broad statement. Jefferson himself, devotee of the dignity of man, would have included Negroes in the free if not the equal status.

Southern Participation in the Shooting War. If Jefferson gave the Revolution its philosophic justification, Washington emerged as the new nation's hero.

Southern states were largely uninvaded until the latter half of the war, though their sons fought in the Contiental army to the northward. Having failed or reached a stalemate in the North, British forces concentrated upon Southern areas. Savannah was captured in 1778, Charleston in 1780. General Horatio Gates, sent south to defy the invaders, met with no success, but Nathanael Greene, who never actually won a battle, provided superior resistance. A convergence of American and French forces, with the aid of a French fleet under Rochambeau, resulted in Lord Cornwallis' capitulation at Yorktown in the fall of 1781. Meanwhile Indians on the southwestern frontier, with British support, ravaged, tortured, and slew frontiersmen and their families, but they succeeded only in delaying the western tide of migration. Tennesseans and Kentuckians firmly held their ground, though in the future some of them would weigh the advantages of attachment to the East or a Southwestern confederacy.

Southern States in the Confederation Period. When the fighting closed at Yorktown, many of the inhabitants of the South, whose lands had been overrun by the British, were impoverished, and the region's economy was dislocated. Economic progress was rapid, however, despite problems of finance and ineffective central government. The South's export products—tobacco, rice, naval stores—were in lesser demand in England, but Continental countries furnished limited markets. If rice recovered more slowly and indigo failed to make a comeback, wheat and flour from the Chesapeake Country showed signs of augmenting regional income.

Southern as well as Northern states circumvented the collection of pre-Revolutionary debts to the British. Internal conflicts over fiat money and taxation created factionalism between radicals and conservatives; and South Carolina's neighbors to the north and south resented that state's import duties. Proposals in Congress to give that body power to regulate internal and foreign commerce created local and sectional jealousy, with Southerners opposing the proposed authority because they believed shipping would be monopolized by North-

ern carriers. Southern delegates resented Northern opposition to pressure that would open the Mississippi to
American navigation.

The problem of commerce was vital in the movement
for a stronger central government. Delegates from
Maryland and Virginia assembled at Mount Vernon to
confer on the navigation of the Potomac; and out of
this conference came a call for a convention at Annapolis to consider the broader aspects of commerce. When
delegates from only five states appeared, the purpose was
abandoned, and another convention was called to meet
at Philadelphia in the spring of 1787 to consider measures that would make the government adequate to the
needs of the new nation.

The South in the Federal Convention. To that
convention Virginia and South Carolina, of the Southern
states, contributed able leaders. Washington became its
president, Madison the Constitution's chief architect,
Edmund Randolph spokesman for the large-state or Virginia plan, George Mason opponent of ratification but
nonetheless a contributor to the constitution's detail and
author of guarantees embodied in the bill of rights
amendments. Charles Cotesworth Pinckney and his
cousin Charles Pinckney, Pierce Butler, John Rutledge
—all South Carolinians—were effective delegates in the
convention's deliberations.

The nationalism of Washington and Madison and
some of the other Southern representatives was manifest in the Virginia proposals. They would, indeed, cir-
cumscribe the powers of the states, but some Southern
proponents of a strong central government were certain
that the South would dominate the new order. At the
same time, Southerners labored for the protection of
their section's interests. They favored counting Negro
slaves in determining representation in the lower house
of Congress; they objected to the assignment of only
twenty-nine of the sixty-five seats in the House to the
Southern states; they favored denying Congress the right
to tax exports or to prohibit immediately the foreign
slave trade. The "federal ratio," whereby 60 per cent of
the slaves would count in determining representation
and direct taxes, would remain a thorn in the flesh of

Northern opponents of slavery. The peculiar institution was recognized, not only in the three-fifths compromise but also in the proviso for rendition of fugitives, though neither the word *slave* nor *slavery* appeared in the organic act.

Ratification by the Southern States. There were sharp debates in Southern conventions over ratification of the Constitution, but Georgia, South Carolina, and Maryland readily approved the document, in the last state with the aid of the stolid Washington. But in Virginia the Anti-Federalist opposition was powerfully aligned behind the eloquence of Patrick Henry, supported by Monroe, Mason, and William Grayson. The cold logic of Madison and his fellow Federalists, Marshall, Edmund Pendleton, and George Nicholas, and the belated shift of Edmund Randolph brought approval by a narrow margin. Only North Carolina of the Southern states defeated ratification; that state delayed approval until after the new Union became a *fait accompli*. In 1789 few Southerners doubted that Virginia would be the keystone of the new nation's arch, or that Southern states would at least maintain an equality in political and economic life.

— 6 —

AGRICULTURAL ECONOMY— AND A LITTLE INDUSTRY

Old and New Staples. Two of the agricultural staples of the colonial era, tobacco and rice, survived the Revolution; indigo failed in the postwar period to re-establish itself in the Southern economy. Cotton and sugar cane, both introduced in the South before the century's turn, became significant factors in the region's economic life, and, like tobacco and rice, affected social, cultural, and political aspects as well.

Sea-Island Cotton.   The Old Rice Coast, from the Santee River to the St. Johns, found a new source of income in the decade following the Revolution. Sea-island cotton arrived first in Georgia from the Bahamas. A limited number of planters in that state and in South Carolina grew this long-fiber cotton which, because of the finer cloth that could be manufactured from it, brought as much as five shillings a pound in the Liverpool market. Exports increased from 1,500,000 pounds in 1790 to 11,000,000 in 1819. Lean years in the thirties and forties were followed by greater productivity in the last ante-bellum decade.

The Cotton Gin and the Cotton Kingdom.   The short-fiber or green-seed variety, rather than sea-island cotton, gave a large part of the South "Cotton Kingdom" status in the ante-bellum era. Before its introduction into the South Carolina–Georgia uplands in the 1790's, slave-holding planters pondered the problem of profit from slave labor. The Virginia Tidewater abandoned tobacco culture in favor of wheat; rice planters viewed the future with uncertainty as they substituted the tide flow for the reservoir system of inundation. Economic forces might have put slavery in the way of ultimate extinction had it not been for the adaptibility of soil, climate, and slave labor to cotton culture—and for Eli Whitney's invention of the cotton gin in 1793. This young, mechanics-minded graduate of Yale College arrived in the South at the propitious moment, seeking a teaching position, not a role as inventor. Invited to the home of Nathanael Greene's widow, he was persuaded by her plantation manager, Phineas Miller, to construct an en-(gin)e that would expedite the separation of lint from seed. He succeeded; and the two formed a partnership to manufacture gins. The partners profited little from the invention because of patent encroachments and resultant litigation, but agriculture had found a mechanical hurdle to a retarding barrier.

Short-Fiber Cotton in the South Carolina–Georgia Piedmont.   The first area that produced short-fiber cotton was the upland of South Carolina and Georgia, with lesser amounts in the Piedmont of Virginia and North Carolina. The deep South Piedmont had accumulated a considerable white population by 1790—over 90,000 in South Carolina alone. Most of the inhabitants were small farmers, though a few owned sufficient slaves to warrant planter status, and prosperous farmers held a limited number. The Piedmont of the lower South remained the important cotton-growing area until the 1820's.

Western Expansion of the Cotton Kingdom. Meanwhile, a newer West beckoned and migrants aplenty—planters as well as farmers—abandoned South Atlantic seaboard states for commonwealths growing up on the Gulf of Mexico. Orleans Territory became Louisiana in 1812; Mississippi entered the Union in 1817 and Alabama two years later. Removal of Indians from western Georgia opened a large area to white settlement. Arkansas was ready for statehood in 1836, and Texas became a part of the American Union a decade later. Departing Virginians and North Carolinians went in about equal numbers to the new Southwest, the immediate West—Kentucky, Tennessee, and Missouri—and the Old Northwest. South Carolinians and Georgians who sought new homes to the westward followed mainly lines of latitude; a few went to the upper South, still fewer to the region north of the Ohio.

The great wave of westward migration that followed the close of the War of 1812 carried slaves as well as whites to the area of rich soil and heavy rainfall that was destined to become the heart of the Cotton Kingdom. But as cotton could be grown profitably on a small as well as a large scale, planters had no monopoly on the staple's production. The cotton belt was not a continuous area from South Carolina west to Arkansas and Texas. By the end of the ante-bellum period, it included the South Carolina Piedmont, middle Georgia, central Alabama and the Huntsville area at the Tennessee's sweep into the northern part of the state, southwestern Tennessee, Mississippi except in its southeastern corner, southern Arkansas, northern Louisiana, and eastern Texas. (*See Document No. 7.*) The greatest expansion of the Cotton Kingdom occurred in the last ante-bellum decade. In 1850 the South grew 2,500,000 bales of the fleecy staple; a decade later, 5,400,000 bales. Two-thirds of the world's supply of raw cotton came from the South on the eve of the Civil War; two-thirds of the Southern crop was produced in the four states of Georgia, Alabama, Mississippi, and Louisiana. The prevailing price of eleven cents a pound in the 1850's gave the Cotton Kingdom a sense of security and prosperity. All other items in the nation's export trade did not total the value of the cotton staple.

Profit from Cotton Beyond the Kingdom. The prosperity of the deep South depended largely upon income from cotton, but other regions and groups also profited from its production. Northern and English shipowners transported cotton bales to New and Old England. Mill owners and their laborers made livelihoods from manufacturing it. Eastern middlemen lined their pockets with commissions. The lower South was obliged to supplement its local food supply by importations from the farming states in the Mississippi, Ohio, and Missouri valleys. A large percentage of the profits from cotton accumulated to the credit of non-Southerners.

Sugar Production in Louisiana. Contemporaneous with the beginnings of cotton in South Carolina and Georgia, Louisiana found a staple in sugar cane. Experimentation with it earlier in the century yielded chiefly negative results, but in the 1790's a Creole, Étienne Boré, grew a crop of cane and manufactured it into sugar worth $12,000. The transfer of Louisiana to the United States and the admission of its southern portion into the Union hastened migration to the area, and the "sugar bowl" rapidly expanded into its ultimate limits—a triangular region with its apex on the Red River in the central part of the state. In the banner year 1853 Louisiana produced 450,000 hogsheads, but production leveled off to half that amount on the eve of the Civil War, which was about 95 per cent of the crop grown in the United States. Texas, Florida, and Georgia grew limited amounts in the ante-bellum period. The market was domestic, with half the product transported to the Eastern seaboard and the other half up the Mississippi River.

One of the great sugar planters was Valcour Aime, whose plantation lay in St. James Parish above New Orleans. By the 1850's the income from his 9,500-acre plantation—manned by over 200 slaves—exceeded $100,000 annually. He was an experimental planter who improved both the agricultural and manufacturing processes—and publicized his findings in agricultural magazines. Some small units existed, but expensive equipment was not conducive to profitable production on a limited scale. Sugar planters were ever tariff conscious to protect their interest from foreign importations, but the price was probably more influenced by the world market than by tariff schedules.

Expansion of the Tobacco Kingdom. Despite abandonment of tobacco culture in Tidewater Virginia, the Tobacco Kingdom expanded in post-Revolutionary years. Maryland's Tidewater remained loyal to the Monarchy, the Old Dominion opened its Piedmont to the staple, and so did adjacent North Carolina. The Kingdom also spread westward over the mountains into Kentucky and Tennessee, and finally into Missouri. The plant spilled over the Ohio River into the Old Northwest, where farmers found it an attractive item in their diverse domestic economy. In Kentucky the famed Bluegrass region, centering about Frankfort and Lexington, and the western third of the state gave it staple rank. Adjacent Tennessee, from the Nashville Basin to the Mississippi River, grew tobacco extensively. And in Missouri, chiefly in the valley north of the Missouri River, the crop reached staple proportions.

The tobacco crop, like cotton, more than doubled in the 1850's. Whether grown by planters with slave labor or by farmers with a few slaves or the labor of the farmer's family, prosperity indicated no fault with the Southern system of economy. Virginia still led in tobacco production as the ante-bellum period drew to a close, but Kentucky and Tennessee had outdistanced North Carolina and Maryland. Missouri stood sixth in production.

The Rice Coast. The area of rice culture remained the same as in the colonial era, with South Carolina, Georgia, and North Carolina, in the order named, its producers. (*See Documents Nos. 8 and 9.*) But unlike tobacco and cotton, the Rice Coast showed signs of deterioration as the Old South reached its heyday. In South Carolina production declined from 160,000,000 pounds in 1850 to 120,000,000 in 1860. Across the Savannah River, production increased slightly in the same decade, from 39,000,000 to 53,000,000 pounds. Louisiana entered the competition in a small way, producing 4,500,-000 pounds in 1850 and more than 6,000,000 in 1860. There it was grown on both sides of the Mississippi in Plaquemines Parish south of New Orleans. In the period of the New South, southwestern Louisiana and parts of Texas and Arkansas would become the great rice-producing area, with artificial flooding and with harvesting methods imported from the upper valley grain states.

Broad Base of the South's Economy. Southern agricultural economy rested on a broader base than the crops associated peculiarly with the South. Of the four distinctive Southern staples, only tobacco had economic significance north of Mason and Dixon's line, where about 14 per cent of the American crop was grown. The Old South also produced an appreciable part of the country's grain and livestock. Amounts increased, but the South lost in relative importance as farmers increased exploitation of the Northwest.

Grain and Minor Crops. According to the census of 1860, the South grew more than half of the nation's corn. Twenty years before, Tennessee and Kentucky ranked first and second as corn-growing states; on the eve of the Civil War they were in sixth and fifth positions. Little was produced for exportation: the border-state surplus was consumed on deep South plantations. The upper South grew 35 per cent of the wheat crop in 1840, but by 1860 the amount declined to 29 per cent of the total. A fifth of the country's rye and oats and four-fifths of its peas and beans were grown in the South. The region produced nearly all of the sweet potatoes, only a tenth of the Irish potatoes. Flax and flax seed were relatively minor items, but 87 per cent of the nation's hemp was grown in Kentucky, Tennessee, and Missouri. In limited parts of these states it reached the rank of a staple; and production at the big bend of the Missouri River, in the same latitude as the Kansas Valley, encouraged proslavery expansionists to hope that Kansas might become a slaveholding state.

Southern Horticulture. Horticulture made significant gains in the ante-bellum period. Charles Michaux, a French botanist, conducted experiments with sundry plants at his botanical garden near Charleston in the late 1700's. A half-century later a transplanted Scotsman, Thomas Affleck, established an enviable reputation as a horticulturist, first in Mississippi and later in Texas. He imported rare plants and trees from Western Europe, experimented with them and native stocks in his nursery, and succeeded in improving Southern economy. Some progress was made in the growing of apples, peaches, oranges, grapes, and figs.

Animal Husbandry. In animal husbandry the South's record was at least promising. All but a tenth of the mule population inhabited the Southern states. Planters theorized that they could stand rough treatment of slaves better than horses, of which Southerners owned 45 per cent. Census reports of 1860 assigned the South three-fifths of the hogs, slightly more than half of the oxen, half of the neat cattle, and about a third of the sheep. The value of its poultry was somewhat more than half of the national total. Commercial dairying produced only a fifth of the butter and a negligible amount of the cheese.

Early Agricultural Reformers: Washington and Jefferson. The myth of agricultural complacency in the Old South was exploded many years ago. Of backward planters and farmers, satisfied with methods and machinery of earlier generations, there were many; but scientific agriculture reduced many economic ills. A growing minority of the rural population was ever alert for better methods of growing crops and means of improving breeds of stock. Among the early reformers were Washington and Jefferson, Virginians genuinely in love with the soil. The master of Mount Vernon conducted fertilizer experiments to enhance soil fertility, practiced rotation of crops, invented and improved farm machinery, corresponded with the English reformer Arthur Young, and avidly read his *Annals of Agriculture*. Jefferson was also an inventor and improver of farm machinery and an experimental agriculturist. He was so thoroughly convinced that toil in the earth developed character that he recommended it to young Americans and advocated introduction of agricultural subjects into the curriculum of his University of Virginia. He saw a relationship between tilling the soil and democratic government, which "could endure only so long as the great majority of the people were farmers."

John Taylor of Caroline and Edmund Ruffin. John Taylor shared Jefferson's enthusiasm for the soil and underscored "agricultural virtues" as a pathway to heaven. He opposed laws that protected and encouraged manufactures and created an artificial "aristocratical order." The ideal republic, he thought, was one in which the great majority would be attached to the soil and control the country's wealth. Like the earlier Virginia agrarians, he experimented and preached what he practiced in books and articles. He was, as Avery Craven indicates, "forging a single program of political philosophy and agricultural practice to prevent the American government from becoming an agent for the plundering of the many by the few; and to keep peasantry from developing on this side of the Atlantic" (*The Coming of the Civil War,* 1942, pp. 46-47). But the Southerner who wrote his name largest in improvement was Edmund Ruffin. A pioneer in soil chemistry, he promoted the use of marl and other fertilizers to improve fertility; and he advocated crop rotation, horizontal and deeper plowing, and proper drainage. His success in increasing corn and wheat yields in his native state resulted in an invitation to become agricultural surveyor of South Carolina. Ruffin's *Essay on Calcareous Manures* and his meritorious magazine, *Farmer's Register* (1833-1843), brought recognition as the foremost reformer in the South.

Southern Nationalism and Independence. Ruffin's goal was twofold: soil improvement to curtail desertion of South Atlantic states by farmers who felt the lure of the West, and Southern economic independence. In the forties and fifties he became a Southern nationalist, a rampant fire-eater who advocated secession and a separate confederacy. Few Southerners shared his separatist ambition until the late fifties. Meanwhile agricultural societies and magazines multiplied. The *Southern Cultivator*, the *Soil of the South*, the *Southern Agriculturist*, *De Bow's Review*, and other periodicals advocated agricultural improvement and economic independence. Eventually, industrial, commercial, and educational independence became rivals of agricultural self-sufficiency.

Southern Industry. The heyday of Southern industrialism arrived in the era of the New South, but the development had unmistakable roots in pre-Civil War years. The last ante-bellum census assigned about 14 per cent of the nation's manufactures to the South. Their value increased substantially in the 1850's: from $142,000,000 to $251,000,000.

The leading industry in 1860 was milling wheat and corn into flour and meal, with Baltimore and Richmond important centers of processing. The value of the Southern output was $56,000,000, 30 per cent of the nation's total. Sawmills that converted yellow pine, live oak, and cypress into lumber, ship timber, shingles, and barrel staves, valued at $25,000,000, ranked second in Southern manufactures, and the Carolina and Georgia forests yielded three-fifths of the turpentine produced in the United States. Maryland, Virginia, Kentucky, and Tennessee engaged in iron manufacture, with Richmond the leading iron-producing city of the Old South. The notable manufacturer in the Virginia capital was Joseph Reid Anderson, who established the Tredegar Iron Works in 1837, operated partly by slave labor. His company manufactured cannon and shells for the government, locomotives for Southern railroads, and steam machinery for sugarhouses in Louisiana.

Ranking with Anderson as a pioneer industrialist in the late ante-bellum period was William Gregg of South Carolina. Like the South's agricultural reformers, he favored "economic liberation," and he also advocated the use of poorer white labor in Southern industry. His cotton textile mill at Graniteville, erected in the late 1840's, became a model for other mills in the Southern Piedmont. Georgia led in cotton manufactures; Maryland, Virginia, North Carolina, and Alabama made small beginnings, but the South's product in 1860, valued at

$11,000,000, was hardly a tenth of the national total. Two of these states, Virginia and North Carolina, pioneered in the manufacture of plug tobacco, processing some two-thirds of their raw product. Regardless of ultimate consumer, tobacco manufacturers sent their output largely to Philadelphia and New York merchants, though a considerable bulk went to California after the Gold Rush. Discovery of gold in North Carolina and Georgia produced no rushes of similar magnitude, though the "gold fever" attracted over six thousand prospectors to Georgia in 1830. Mines in those and other southern Appalachian states yielded bullion worth over $5,000,000 between 1824 and 1837.

As a sampling of minor industries, the Old South manufactured agricultural implements, beer and whiskey, salt, wool, leather goods, buggies and carriages, and cotton bagging and rope from its hemp supply. The reaper, invented by the Virginia-born Cyrus Hall McCormick, eventually found its industrial habitat in Chicago, center of the upper valley grain-growing country.

Agriculture and industry, whether in simple or complex economy, require commercial connections with neighboring and distant communities. It seems appropriate to turn to certain aspects of trade and transportation in the Old South.

— 7 —

TRADE AND TRANSPORTATION

Interdependence of Planters, Slave Traders, and Commission Merchants. The professional slave trader, the commission merchant, and the Southern planter were inseparably associated in the exploitation of agricultural resources in the ante-bellum South. The business of all three was so interdependent that one could not operate successfully without the existence of the other two. The planter engaged in large-scale agriculture; he depended upon the slave trader to provide Negro laborers to cultivate his expanding acres, and he relied upon the factor to market his crops, to furnish plantation supplies, and to supply credit. He attended to all sorts of requests, from errand boy to supplying the planter's wife with cash when she sojourned in the city to replenish her wardrobe and attend the opera. Without the planter, the country business of the commission merchant would have been of minor significance. Insofar as the slave trader was responsible for the presence of Negroes in any region he contributed an element that produced much of the raw material shipped to the factor and consumed much of the goods provided for plantation use. Credit with factorage firms enabled the planter to purchase slaves; not infrequently he paid for them with promissory notes drawn upon urban countinghouses.

The Foreign Slave Trade. Until the closing of the foreign sources in 1808, an adequate supply of slaves was available in importations from Africa and the West Indies. Even after the congressional exclusion act went into effect, an uncertain volume of illicit traffic continued, but it was not sufficient to affect materially the domestic trade. And, in spite of sundry voices raised in favor of reopening the foreign sources, congressional prohibition continued throughout the ante-bellum period, and the Confederate Constitution left the situation unchanged.

Community Slave Trade. Historically, the domestic traffic in slaves existed on a small scale in the colonial period, but it was more or less incidental until the eighteenth century faded into the nineteenth. Of the two varieties, community and long distance, the first was accomplished by personal notices of surpluses for disposal, newspaper advertisements, and public auctions. A large volume of trade was handled by auctioneers in such cities as Baltimore, Richmond, Charleston, Savannah, and New Orleans. They charged a commission on sales, usually 2½ per cent, and a daily rate of 37½ cents for maintaining a slave until sold.

Long-Distance Slave Trade. The long-distance slave trade was an important phase of the westward movement. Planters and farmers, seeking new homes in the West, carried slaves with them, and occasionally returned to purchase others to till increasing acreages. The professional slave trader, however, was largely responsible for transporting a surplus of slaves from the older to newer portions of the South. In the early 1800's the Chesapeake area sent many to the upcountry of South Carolina and Georgia. The great volume of slave traffic following the close of the War of 1812 was from northeast to southwest: from Virginia, Maryland, and the District of Columbia to new commonwealths developing on the Gulf of Mexico. The demand in the new Southwest was greater than the supply, slave prices soared, and large profits in the traffic gave rise to the professional slave trader. His equipment consisted of a slave pen in the exporting states in which slaves purchased in the surrounding area were assembled for the journey to the Southwest, means of transportation to selling markets, and a distributing center for their disposal.

The Buying Area. Although there were few slaves in the District of Columbia, it was situated in the center of an important buying market. The trade thrived in Georgetown and Alexandria as well as in the nation's capital. Location on the Potomac expedited coastwise shipment to South Atlantic and Gulf ports. By the end of the ante-bellum period, sixty or seventy traders, auctioneers, and agents dealt in Negroes at Richmond; others utilized Petersburg, Warrenton, Lynchburg, Norfolk, Baltimore, Frederick, and Easton on the Eastern Shore. Prohibition of the trade in the District at mid-century enhanced the trade at Baltimore as well as at Alexandria. Taverns and jails served many traders as places of detention while the assembling process was in progress; others maintained slave pens of their own.

Means of Transporting Slaves to Distant Markets. By the middle of the nineteenth century there were four methods of transporting slaves to distant markets. Schooners and brigs plied the coastwise traffic, river-boats utilized the Mississippi and its tributaries, railroads provided crude passenger, baggage, and freight cars, and overland coffles followed the roads and traces traveled by migrating planters and farmers. The alternative employed was largely determined by destination: slaves bound for an inland market were usually sent overland, by river, or by railroad; those consigned to port towns were forwarded coastwise. From October to May fast-sailing packet brigs bearing cargoes of seventy-five to two hundred slaves made a half-dozen or more trips, carrying perhaps three thousand Negroes annually. Second in importance to coastwise traffic was overland transportation. Slave coffles varied greatly in size, but three hundred was a maximum. Some slaves were peddled to townsmen and planters along the way, but most of them continued to such inland centers as Columbus, Montgomery, Jackson, and Natchez. A much-traveled route lay through southwestern Virginia and the valley of East Tennessee, whence it led by various routes into Georgia, Alabama, and Mississippi. Averaging twenty to twenty-five miles a day, a slave coffle made the trip from the Chesapeake area to the Mississippi River in seven or eight weeks.

The Selling Market. Transient venders peddled their property in huckster fashion; the resident trader maintained a slave pen to which planters, farmers, and merchants resorted to inspect his wares. The "mistress of the trade" was New Orleans, the greatest slave emporium of the Southwest. (*See Document No. 10.*) Hundreds of traders engaged in the trade there in the generation preceding the Civil War. At the sound of bell or other signal in the slave pens of established venders, the males and females, a few of the latter with babes in arms, speedily formed into two lines according to height. The attendant inquired what type of slave the customer desired, and made his recommendation accordingly. Age, sex, skill, physical and mental qualities were factors in determining the price, though haggling occasionally resulted in reduction for buyers who drove a hard bargain. Curious travelers were more interested in public auctions at the St. Charles and St. Louis Hotels, where professional auctioneers combined salesmanship and wit in a constant flow of French and English jargon.

The Slave Trader in Public Opinion. The slave trade and the slave trader were viewed with mixed emotions by contemporaries of the Old South. The traffic was tolerated as a necessity, much as it was outwardly regretted. A great many planters were opposed to selling slaves as a matter of principle, and thus accumulated through natural increase more than strict economic necessity warranted. But lack of economic opportunity in the older South, financial reverses, and the settling of estates necessitated disposal of slave property. "Nigger traders," often alluded to as sharpers by contemporaries, were ostracized in Southern society. Commission merchants of Baltimore, Richmond, Charleston, and New Orleans were ordinarily respectable citizens who were quite willing to accommodate their clients by attending to the sale of a few slaves, charging of course a substantial commission. No publicity was given to such transactions, and neither planters nor factors suffered as a result. Resident professional traders were often in good social standing, especially if they were in business on a generous scale and invested profits in the legitimate business of planting.

Isaac Franklin accumulated the most of a million-dollar estate in the long-distance slave trade, much of which he invested in land and Negroes in Tennessee and Louisiana. His home plantation "Fairview" in the Bluegrass region of Tennessee rivaled the "Hermitage" in the eyes of Tennesseans, and his several plantations in West Feliciana Parish, Louisiana, made him one of the great cotton barons of the Lower South. Nathan Bedford Forrest, Confederate cavalry leader, gained the respect of his Southern contemporaries in spite of his participation in the slave trade, but he, like Franklin, was attached to the soil.

River Transportation. As means of internal transportation, the South built a few canals in the thirties and forties. The region was fortunate in its river systems which brought products from the interior to port cities. The Cotton Kingdom in particular was well served by waterways, among them the Savannah, Alabama-Tombigbee, and Mississippi. (*See Document No. 11.*) With pardonable pride acclamatory New Orleanians witnessed the agricultural surplus of the Mississippi Valley deposited in their city. A vast hinterland, they said, was served by "a great spinal cord" and its tributaries that provided twenty thousand miles of navigation. More than three score products valued at a hundred million dollars in 1850 were deposited on the city's levee and in its warehouses. The great Southern staples, cotton, sugar, molasses, and tobacco, were worth seventy-two millions; and if minor items be included, Southern states in the valley accounted for three-fourths of the total. The meat- and grain-producing states sent most of the remainder, with their corn, oats, wheat, and flour worth six and a half millions, and their lard, bacon, and pork valued at thirteen and a half. Watercraft of every description—keelboats, barges, and flatboats, brigs, schooners, and sloops—anchored there, some engaged in the river trade, others in the coastwise and foreign traffic.

Railroad Transportation. The era of the railroads gave Atlantic coastal cities better opportunity to compete for commercial supremacy and at the same time to contribute toward the development of inland trade. Private enterprise by individuals and companies, aided and supplemented by city, county, and state governments, built some ten thousand miles of track by 1860, nearly a third of the nation's mileage. By that time there were three main east-west lines, a half-dozen north-south lines, and a network of local feeders to the "trunk" lines. Baltimore profited most from railroad building by tapping the Ohio and Mississippi valleys. Whereas that city and New Orleans were about equal in population at mid-century, Baltimore grew to 212,000 in 1860, New Orleans to 169,000.

Southern Exports and Northern Profits. Southern economy was severely handicapped by a lack of working capital. In contrast with the free North, much Southern capital was tied up in a source of labor supply. Agricultural profits were invested in more slaves and more acres to produce more staple crops. These were shipped from Southern ports to western Europe, or to the Northeast, or sometimes to England by way of New York. But the ships that departed with Southern staples did not return laden with manufactured goods. They brought goods to Eastern cities, whither Southern merchants resorted to purchase supplies. The value of Southern exports greatly exceeded imports; the reverse was true of New York City. Why should Southerners contribute to the wealth of the Northeast by middlemen's commissions, additional freight charges—and tariffs?

Commercial Conventions. The South sought an answer to that question in commercial conventions, a means it used as early as the thirties. Between 1853 and 1859 eight more conventions assembled in leading Southern cities, each one calling the next before it adjourned. Delegates discussed a dozen or more subjects, but the important themes were a Pacific railroad, opening the Amazon River Valley to Southern trade, direct commerce with Europe, and educational improvement. The tariff inevitably stirred debate, but the moderate schedules of the Walker enactment of 1846 were satisfactory to most Southerners. They resented exceedingly the necessity of European importations by way of Eastern cities. And they resented also Northern control over the Southern mind. Schoolbooks should be written by Southerners, and the South should establish a great printing house to free the section from dependence upon Northern publishers. Tangible results were negligible, but the conventions gave delegates opportunity to vocalize their views on means of protecting Southern rights.

SOCIETY IN THE ANTE-BELLUM SOUTH

Southern Society in Travel Accounts. Hundreds of travelers in the Old South—from the North and from European countries—put pens to paper and left permanent records of their impressions. Observers of the Southern scene ranged all the way from physicians and scientists through teachers and preachers to farmers and soldiers. Sightseers and healthseekers also came; and they like their contemporaries with serious purpose found employment for their pens. Society and institutions, particularly slavery, interested casualist as well as expert. (*See Documents No. 12 and 13.*) Some travelers also toured the North and found occasion to compare the sections. Many traveled fast and furiously but nevertheless posed as authorities. At the other extreme, visitors sojourned here and there for weeks or months, and thus remained long enough to give more validity to their observations. Some came with their minds already fixed and sought only confirming evidence of predilections. Wherever travelers went, they found "characters" who provided spice to enliven their narratives. (*See Document No. 14.*)

An Alabama Reply. Wth some notable exceptions, visitors emphasized three social classes: planters, poor whites, and slaves. Daniel R. Hundley, an Alabama "sociologist," published *Social Relations in Our Southern States* in 1860 to inform outsiders of their errors. With unfortunate irritation emerging from many pages, he classified Southerners by identifying gentlemen, middle classes, Southern Yankees, cotton snobs, yeomen, bullies, poor white trash, and Negro slaves. While Hundley's classification has been considerably modified by histo-

rians, he correctly identified several distinct groups between great planters and poor whites. The Alabama
writer resented most the Northern view that there were
no yeomen in the South. In "speech, religious opinions,
household arrangements, indoor sports, and family tradi-
tions," he insisted, they resembled Northern farmers. He
reserved his greatest contempt for the cotton snob, who
had his counterpart in the North and often strutted at
watering places in both sections "flirting with senseless
girls." Superficially educated, the snob was "valiant and
chivalrous, when under the influence of two or three
Brandy Straights, and as many Cocktails." His chief interests were "wine and women, women and wine, fast
nags, splendid trotters, New York buggies—hurrah!"

Historical Account of Social Classes. Hundley's
multiple-class theme has been developed historically in
recent years from tax lists and manuscript census reports
that indicate personal properties as well as acreages.
Ante-bellum Southern society, Frank L. Owsley discovered, was normal and healthy. Cavaliers were not "the
great monopolists of their day"; nor were the six or seven
million nonslaveholding inhabitants of the poor "white
trash" variety. There were planters, large and small,
farmers with three or four hundred acres and a few
slaves, nonslaveholding farmers with a hundred or two
acres, and "one-horse farmers" with less land. There
were also farmers who hired laborers to till several hundred acres; and there were squatters and renters and
farmhands. "But the core of the social structure was a
massive body of plain folk who were neither rich nor
very poor. These were employed in numerous occupations; but the great majority secured their food, clothing, and shelter from some rural pursuit, chiefly farming
and livestock grazing" (*Plain Folk of the Old South*,
1949, pp. 7-8).

Popular Conception of the Plantation. If ante-
bellum travelers distorted Southern society by observing
only planters, poor whites, and slaves, that tradition was
carried forward in literature, on the stage, and in popular song. The moonlight and magnolia concept portrayed
the Old South as an idyllic society of beautiful women
and gracious gentlemen; of happy, carefree slaves who

toiled long hours in the fields but sang and played on warm starlit evenings, chanting spirituals and amusing themselves with rude sports. Ordinarily missing from the picture were the unfortunate poor whites who led listless lives, dipped snuff, drank hard liquor, and eked out a precarious existence on marginal land, whose misery and degradation might have provided contrast to underscore the luster of the privileged class. In actuality, the idyllic fades into reality in the cold light of history. Romanticism was apparent here and there, but so was the hard life of farming, of perverse weather, of uncomfortable travel, of pellagra and malaria, of selfish politicians, of economic adversity.

Genteel Living. Only a few of the planters lived in white-columned mansions, but the few were enough to establish a tradition. Travelers sought and often received invitations to tarry for a visit, and thus witnessed gracious living in a cultured environment. A half-dozen house servants served as coachmen and cooks, nursemaids and housekeepers, houseboys and valets. Such slaves occupied privileged positions on the plantation and formed an elite class who were condescending to the less fortunate fieldhands. Skilled laborers, often though not always mulattoes, were trained as carpenters and coopers, masons and tanners, wheelwrights and blacksmiths. They, too, had privileges not accorded the men and women who labored with plow and hoe in the fields or harvested the crops of tobacco, cotton, sugar, and rice.

The mansion itself, with spacious high-ceilinged rooms upstairs and down, provided an atmosphere of genteel quality and leisurely living. Daily routine varied with the planter's habits of life and work. Some must be up early to make the rounds of the plantation on horseback, visiting the gangs of laborers in the field or workers at ginhouse or mill. Others, like the Mississippian, Thomas S. Dabney, rose late, with the assurance that overseer and drivers had the hands at work by sunup. Visitors must amuse themselves in library or music room, or in strolling over the spacious yard or down the avenue of trees, lined with statuary imported from France or Italy, that led from the mansion to the road. Dinner at four, often preceded by mint juleps on the broad piazza, was an occasion that no one missed. Evenings on the front gallery, or in the living room in bad weather, were gala occasions with cards and dancing, or chitchat about crops and weather and tariffs. Social life in the grand manner was an impressive experience for tourists and sojourners.

Lesser Aristocracy. More often the plantation house was a modest frame structure of a story and a half with less spacious rooms and ordinary furnishings. The planter personally supervised the labor of his fifty or seventy-five slaves, especially if he had competent drivers. An avenue of trees might lead to the house, but it was not lined with statuary, and the house itself might present a run-down appearance. Of house servants there were fewer; of generous living, less. The planter might enjoy a measure of prosperity, and sons might be sent to college and girls to finishing schools.

Farmers and Poorer Whites. Farmers with a few slaves or none lived in unkept houses that belied their middle-class position in Southern society. The farmer and his sons made hands on the farm in less routine labor than the plantation system demanded. Perhaps a man-servant or a maidservant gave part time to household duties, especially if there were small children, but social stratification could hardly exist among so small a laboring force. On the frontier, or on marginal land occupied by families living precariously in near self-sufficient economy, squalor emphasized primitive existence and illiteracy. (*See Document No. 15.*) Such families had little to wear and a monotonous diet, though the forlorn traveler, far off the course of opulence, would be welcome to humble fare. Log-cabin inmates were plentiful in backwoods and mountain coves—people far from the currents of thought and action.

Travel: European and Domestic. The socially elite of the Old South found diversion in travel at home and abroad. A trip to Cuba brought relief from summer languor; an Atlantic crossing lent gaiety aboard ship and opportunity to meet England's aristocracy. Romanticism prompted a visit to the home of Sir Walter Scott, whose novels gave Southerners flights of fancy to a land of make-believe. A tour of France and Spain provided table talk and parlor patter for future years. Men steeped in the classics found in Athens and Rome the ultimate in civilization; dilettantes found a superficial prestige and a refurbished veneer.

Only a few of the elite toured Europe. The others found recourse in summer vacations nearer home. Planters of Louisiana, Mississippi, and Alabama frequented Pass Christian, Bay St. Louis, Biloxi, Gulfport, or Mobile on the Gulf Coast. Mississippi Valley aristocrats sojourned in New Orleans, or sent their wives and daughters there for social whirls and shopping sprees. The lecherously intriguing French Quarter, on "the other side" of Canal Street, made the Crescent City America's most interesting metropolis. Planters and their families from the Rice Coast frequented Charleston, as we have seen, and that ancient city attracted tourists from a wide area.

Of the Virginia Springs—Greenbrier, Sweet, Hot, Warm, Red Sulphur, and White Sulphur—the last was the ultimate in social prestige. Situated in a valley of the Allegheny Mountains in present-day West Virginia, the White Sulphur was the most fashionable and exclusive. A large hotel accommodated vacationers, though some gentlemen who came year after year built their own cottages or log houses on surrounding hills. Hundreds of visitors took their meals at the hotel, where board cost eight dollars a week. The major-domo proprietor, whose annual receipts were fifty thousand dollars, accommodated only the best "known" families. Therapeutic qualities of the sulphured water were widely advertised, but more visitors came for pleasure than for health. If dinners were bad, lack of quality was attributed to the problem of serving seven hundred people in one dining room. Men talked politics; mothers and their daughters turned an eye in the direction of eligible matches. (*See Document No. 16.*)

The Common Man's Diversions. Middle-class folk seldom traveled to coastal towns or watering places for vacations, but they and their less fortunate contemporaries on frontier or poor land found diversions within smaller radius. Muster days, court sessions, political campaigns, camp meetings, frolics with folk games peculiar to the locality, and Sunday meeting with dinner on the grounds provided relief from the monotony and tedium of everyday living. All except the last—and it was not always an exception—might result in peripheral arguments that did not await the course of the law in courts of justice. Among the rowdy riffraff, fisticuffs, gouging of eyes, chewing off of ears, and other rough-and-tumble displays of physical prowess attracted crowds of eager watchers who registered shouting applause for skill and dexterity. Rural taverns, city grogshops, and river-boat landings were often scenes of shooting affrays.

Satisfaction of Honor: The Duel. The aristocracy had other means of satisfying honor. Dueling, an importation from Western Europe with medieval origins, prevailed in the colonies and continued into the national period in all sections of the United States. The custom became firmly fixed in the South, with Spanish and French influences, emphasis on individualism, and planter class chivalry motivating resort to the field of honor. Swords in the colonial era, pistols in the post-Revolutionary period, were the usual weapons, but use was also made of rifles and shotguns, Bowie knives and swordcanes, lances and harpoons. Trivial differences of opinion, real or fancied wrongs and insults, frequently involving "southern womanhood," led men to settle them by the code. Ordinarily they were serious affairs, with much attention to arrangements by seconds, though not without touches of humor as in the case of the thin man and his oversize opponent. Difference in stature was adjusted by drawing lines on the corpulent duelist representing the width of his opponent; bullets that landed outside the lines did not count—for the satisfaction of honor. Dueling declined after the Civil War. The carnage of conflict and the economic ruin of planters hastened its disappearance.

Purpose of Education in the South. The Southern concept of education was training for leadership. With this goal, public elementary education languished, at least until the closing years of the ante-bellum period. On the other hand, academies and colleges flourished. Most of the South's great leaders attended one or both, and for that time many of them were well educated.

Elementary Education. The South came belatedly to recognize education as a state responsibility, though the error is often made of supposing that there were no free public elementary schools before the Civil War. Tutors were still used in many communities (*see Document No. 17*), but the problem of indigent children eventually forced reluctant public action, stimulated in part by the "common man" philosophy of the Jacksonian period. South Carolina, in fact, provided in 1811 for free schools. Open to all children, preference was given to indigents. Other states in the forties and fifties made educational facilities optional with local districts. The 600,000 pupils attending 18,000 schools in 1860 indicate a beginning, but comparative illiteracy statistics reveal an Old South that lagged far behind the Northeast and somewhat behind the Northwest.

Academies. On the other hand, the South boasted 3,000 academies with some 300,000 students by the last ante-bellum decade. A few of them, such as Waddell's Academy at Willington, South Carolina, and Liberty Hall in Virginia attained enviable reputations. Whether secular or denominational, their curriculums included the classics, and they did not neglect literary and scientific subjects. Considerable attention was given to the physical and biological sciences.

Colleges and Universities. At the higher education level—often secondary in reality—there were 260 colleges and universities in the South in 1860, with 1,500 teachers providing instruction that ranged from mediocrity to excellence for 25,000 students. Denominational colleges predominated. The first state university in the South—North Carolina—began in 1795; Georgia and South Carolina a few years later. The University of Virginia, largely Jefferson's handiwork, opened its doors in the middle twenties; and before the ante-bellum period closed, Alabama, Tennessee, Mississippi, and Louisiana inaugurated state institutions. Under the leadership of Horace Holley, Transylvania gained recognition as a superior school in the 1820's; and Thomas Cooper gave

South Carolina College stature in that decade and the next.

"Female" Education. The schools already discussed were for men only; and while the South, as other sections of the country, was less interested in educating women, "female" academies and institutes were numerous on Southern soil. These "finishing schools" provided opportunity to master social graces. Ancient and modern languages were standard parts of their curriculums, but "sweet Southern girls" also studied astronomy, botany, chemistry, geography, geology, mineralogy, and natural philosophy.

The Spoken Word Versus the Printed Page. The public forum in the South—political gatherings, the courts, religious meetings—supplemented schools as avenues to learning. The spoken word more than the printed page moulded sentiment, directed thought, and aroused enthusiasm. Among the popular spell-binding orators were Seargent S. Prentiss of Mississippi and William L. Yancey of Alabama. The cold logic of Calhoun was wearisome to listeners—his deep abstract reasoning exhausted the 450-pound Senator Dixon H. Lewis. But the South Carolinian's published treatises demonstrated a philosophical competence equaled by few Americans of his day. Public libraries experienced remarkable growth in the 1850's; their holdings in that decade grew fivefold. Still, Southerners were not, generally speaking, a reading people. The ratio of books to white citizens in 1860 was one to every two or three.

Newspapers and Magazines. Ante-bellum Southerners wrote and read little "literature," but they excelled in their highly politicalized press. From fifteen newspapers at the close of the Revolution, the number increased to six hundred by 1850, sixty-seven of which were dailies. For able editing and wide influence, Thomas Ritchie's Democratic Richmond *Enquirer* outranked all other papers. Robert Barnwell Rhett's Charleston *Mercury*, state right's advocate, George D. Prentice's Louisville *Journal*, Unionist adherent, and George W. Kendall's New Orleans *Picayune*, nonpartisan in its early years, represented varying types of Southern journalism. Of Southern magazines, many died a-borning and most of the others lasted only a few years. The greatest of them was the Richmond *Southern Literary Messenger* (1834-1864), which numbered Edgar Allan Poe among its editors and contributors and maintained considerable quality. Charleston's literary ambitions inaugurated over thirty periodicals between the Revolution and the Civil War, but its most successful magazine was the *Southern Quarterly Review,* which acquired some literary merit in the early fifties under the editorship of William Gilmore Simms. From 1846 until the third year of the war, and sporadically thereafter, James D. B. De Bow's *Commercial Review of the South and West,* published in New Orleans, attempted coverage of literature, internal improvements, manufactures, and agriculture as well as trade and commerce. Southern subscribers lived chiefly in the cotton states; New York and Philadelphia merchants and bankers found it useful.

Realism and Romanticism. Southern realism found expression in such humorous publications as Joseph G. Baldwin's *Flush Times of Alabama and Mississippi,* Augustus Baldwin Longstreet's *Georgia Scenes,* and J. J. Hooper's *Adventures of Captain Simon Suggs.* Their rollicking, boisterous tales exhibited down-to-earth characterizations unattained in romantic fiction. Yet John Pendleton Kennedy's historical novels, *Horseshoe Robinson* and *Rob of the Bowl,* and his satirical *Swallow Barn* earned well-merited recognition. The prolific romancer Simms wrote history and biography as well as novels fast and furiously, and while his polemics stanchly defended his state and region, South Carolina aristocracy restrained its enthusiasm for his work. Among his better novels were *Guy Rivers, The Yemassee,* and *The Partisan* of the 1830's and *Katherine Walton, The Forayers,* and *Eutau* of the 1850's. Only by courtesy could his verse be called poetry. Good poets were scarce, but Richard Henry Wilde's "My Life Is Like the Summer Rose" and Theodore O'Hara's "The Bivouac of the Dead" had enduring qualities. Associated with Simms in Charleston literary endeavors were Paul Hamilton Hayne and Henry Timrod, poets who contributed to the *Southern Literary Messenger* and Charleston's *Russell's Magazine.* Edgar Allan Poe, his southernism disputed, attained lasting reputation in "Annabel Lee," in his lines "To Helen," and in sundry short stories.

Simms's biographer, William P. Trent, theorized that his subject in particular and his region in general produced no great literature because slavery shackled the mind and repressed imagination. Writing in thralldom's shadow, Southerners still lived in a feudal atmosphere that prevented a wholesome intellectual activity. The evil effects of slavery in this premise can hardly be doubted. Had Trent understood ante-bellum society in all of its diversity, he might have discovered moments of normality when conflict, internal and external, was relegated to the periphery of attention, and inhabitants pursued vocation and avocation in nonmilitant mood. Some of the more controversial aspects of Southern history, especially in the realms of politics and slavery, await consideration.

— 9 —

FROM JEFFERSON TO JACKSON: POLITICS AND MINORITY SELF-CONSCIOUSNESS

Minority Self-Consciousness. Writers have experienced much disagreement as to when the South became conscious of itself. A few evidences indicate a realization of differences in the colonial era, but they were the normal experiences of people living in different areas. A generation ago a writer traced the South as a conscious minority back to the Federal Convention of 1787. From that time until 1860, he said, the South was constantly struggling to protect minority rights in the Union, with chief reliance upon local government in the period before the Missouri controversy, upon the concurrent voice between the compromises of 1820 and 1850, and upon constitutional guarantees in the last ante-bellum decade. Finally, in 1860, it resorted to a stroke for Southern independence (Jesse T. Carpenter, *The South as a Conscious Minority,* 1930).

Considerable evidence fits into this neat pattern, but it would be difficult to define the South in terms of militant defense of minority rights before 1820. In population, of course, the South was a minority, and therefore it had fewer members in the House of Representatives and fewer votes in the Electoral College. In the Senate a balance was maintained until the admission of California in 1850. Southern and Western collaboration in the early years of the nineteenth century relegated the Northeast to a minority role, with efforts in the Hartford Convention to protect its minority position. In some respects the South shared nearly equally the responsibility of government. Between 1789 and 1861, nine out of fifteen presidents were from the South (for about fifty years of the seventy-two); and the section furnished six of the fourteen vice-presidents, twenty-nine of the thirty-seven justices of the Supreme Court, seventy-three of one hundred fifty-three members of the cabinets, twelve of twenty-three speakers of the House of Representatives, and forty-seven of eighty-two diplomats to England, France, Russia, Spain, and Austria.

Federalist and Republican Parties.   The first political cleavage after the Constitution went into effect was an East-West division. The Northeast eventually became the last stronghold of Federalism, but in the 1790's the party had considerable strength among Tidewater planters who saw virtue in Hamilton's program of centralism and nationalism. A democratic aristocrat, Jefferson, led back country forces of small farmers and frontiersmen against commercial and planting wealth from New England to Georgia. The erudite scholar whose understanding of science, philosophy, and the classics was superior, whose architectural talent was widely recognized, whose emancipatory and educational ideas outdistanced most contemporary thought, and whose plantation home in the foothills of the Blue Ridge was a mecca for travelers native and European, succeeded by the century's turn in capturing the presidency and Congress for the Republican party. Localism in government, the free and equal status of men, religious freedom, and faith in the agricultural masses sparked the Revolution of 1800.

Kentucky and Virginia Resolutions. One of the early manifestations of minority protection found expression in state resolutions. The Alien and Sedition Acts of 1798 seemed clearly unconstitutional to Republicans and some Federalists. Jefferson and Madison protested against them in the Kentucky and Virginia Resolutions. In attacking the constitutionality of this extreme legislation, the resolutions asserted the compact theory of the Union, reminded Americans that the general government had only such powers as the Constitution delegated to it, reserving all other powers to the states or to the people, and underscored freedom of speech, press, and religion. A second set of Kentucky Resolutions was more explicit: the rightful remedy for federal usurpation of power was nullification by state sovereignties. (*See Document No. 18.*) While the resolutions expressed constitutional interpretation, their immediate purpose was to publicize the extreme position of the Federalist party. In a limited sense they served as an embryonic political platform in Republican preparation for the election of 1800.

Jeffersonian Philosophy and Policy. The Revolution of 1800 was not institutional: the constructive work of the Federalists was not destroyed. Social and ethical currents ran in new channels. The party of the rich and the wellborn gave way to one with a political philosophy that would diffuse power among a larger body of the citizenry. Jefferson's first inaugural, a document that ranks with both of Lincoln's and Wilson's first for literary craftsmanship as well as for democratic credo, merits quoting. The Virginia liberal phrased his principles in well-chosen words: "Equal and exact justice to all men," friendship and trade with other countries, "support of the State governments in all their rights," majority rule, "the supemacy of the civil over the military authority," public economy to lighten labor's burden, "encouragement of agriculture, and of commerce as its handmaid," freedom of person, press, and religion, "and trial by juries impartially selected." Jefferson defined "a wise and frugal Government" as one "which shall restrain men from injuring one another, shall leave them otherwise free to regulate their own industry and improvement, and shall not take from the mouth of labor the bread it has earned."

Theorist and idealist in his principles, Jefferson was practical in his politics. He could see farther west than most of his contemporaries: hence sponsorship of Lewis and Clark's expedition to the Far West; hence also, and of more immediate consequence, the purchase of Louisiana despite his own and Federalists' constitutional objections. That acquisition placed his administration on a national basis and added to his stature with Southerners and Westerners. The Virginian performed so adequately in the presidency that there was little opposition to his re-election, even among Federalists.

The Jeffersonian party established a Virginia–New York alliance that made Aaron Burr its candidate for the vice-presidency in 1800 and George Clinton in the two following contests. But by 1808 a rift developed: "Tertium Quids," particularly strong in Virginia and North Carolina, preferred Monroe to Madison as Jefferson's successor. Led by John Randolph, John Taylor, and Nathaniel Macon, they became dissatisfied with Jeffersonianism: it violated state rights by promoting the national authority, as in the acquisition of Louisiana and the embargo policy. Despite opposition of Quids in the South and weariness with the Virginia Dynasty in the North, Jefferson's choice, Secretary of State Madison, became his successor.

Madison and the War Hawks. Jefferson's great collaborator found the sailing rough, but muddled through his eight years in the presidency with considerable courage and a modicum of success. Politically, his first term was marked by the rise of the War Hawks within his own party—young Southerners and Westerners who demanded an aggressive policy against England and France for their encroachments upon American neutral rights at sea. The congressional election of 1810 sent such younger men as Clay, Calhoun, and Felix

Grundy to the lower house, who seized control and elected Clay to the speakership. They were nationalists and expansionists who looked with covetous eyes upon Canada and the Floridas. South Carolina as well as Kentucky leadership was apparent. Calhoun headed the Committee on Foreign Affairs; William Lowndes, Naval Affairs; and Langdon Cheves, Ways and Means. War Hawks looked on with misgivings when the New England minority, which had much to lose from war with England and admission of Louisiana into the Union, expressed sectional sentiment. Protests of the Hartford Convention, and the more radical views of New England extremists, were not unlike the fears expressed by Southerners when their section became a protesting minority in the next generation.

Nationalism, 1812 and After.   A stronger wave of nationalism engulfed the nation—and the party of Jefferson—with the close of the War of 1812. Appropriations for more adequate national defense and legislation that created a second national bank and inaugurated a policy of protecting industry were signed by a president who had led the opposition to Hamilton's broad program of the 1790's. In one important instance Madison drew the yardstick of strict construction: he vetoed the internal improvements or Bonus Bill, demanding an amendment to the Constitution before Congress appropriated federal funds for roadbuilding. It is impressive to note Calhoun's nationalistic qualities in this era. He shared with Clay leadership that sponsored the bank and tariff acts of 1816. In advocating the tariff bill he anticipated Webster's famous reply to Hayne by fourteen years: the Massachusetts Senator in 1830 happily combined the words *liberty, union,* and *inseparable* in eloquent juxtaposition. Calhoun, in 1816, told his House colleagues that "the liberty and union of this country were inseparably united." The South Carolinian was not disturbed over the constitutionality of the internal improvements bill. It would, he counseled, counteract the danger of disunion. The future of the nation seemed rosy to the nationalist who would eventually become a sectionalist.

Monroe and Party Harmony.   Jefferson's party, with change in personnel and policy, had outfederalized the Federalists, and the unpopular Hartford Convention assured the demise of the party of Hamilton. The last of the Virginia Dynasty, James Monroe, succeeded Madison in the presidency without organized opposition. The young Calhoun accepted a place in the cabinet as secretary of war, and effectively reorganized that department. William Crawford, Virginia-born Georgian, was continued as secretary of the treasury; the brilliant Virginia lawyer, William Wirt, was appointed attorney general; and the well-sired and experienced John Quincy Adams was designated secretary of state so that Monroe could not be accused of naming his successor in the presidency. The cabinet was strong and harmonious despite divergent sectional and economic views of Republicans who composed it; despite also sectional tension that emanated from the Missouri crisis.

The Missouri Controversy. The controversy over Missouri's recognition as a state was an important step in developing a Southern self-consciousness. The Senate debate over its admission involved a constitutional question on the nature of the Union. The restrictionists, led by Rufus King of New York, underscored the phrase "may be admitted" from the provision that read, "New States may be admitted by the Congress into this Union." Since Congress could deny admission it could also place qualifications. The nonrestrictionists, whose spokesman was William Pinkney of Maryland, emphasized the expression "into this Union," insisting that if Missouri were admitted with a slavery restriction, the Union would be transformed into one of unequal states. Missouri was admitted without a slavery restriction; the remainder of the Louisiana Purchase territory north of 36° 30' would be forever free. Sectional balance in the Senate was maintained by the admission of Maine. The debate in both houses publicized an embarrassing issue between the sections. It revealed a problem that would grow in intensity during the next forty years and that would seem increasingly irrepressible to extremists.

Election of 1824-1825. The party of Jefferson had become by Monroe's "Era of Good Feeling" an all-embracing structure, indicated by Monroe's nearly unanimous re-election to the presidency in 1820. Pockets of

Federalism remained here and there in the Northeast, and a few members of Congress and local officeholders still paraded under the Hamiltonian cognomen. In this period of personal politics two Southerners, Calhoun and Crawford, sought the succession; and so did Clay and Jackson, slaveholders whose westernism was fully as pronounced as their southernism. Adams showed surprising strength, and with Clay's help won the prize in the House contest of 1825. The New Englander had considerable support in the South, but his strength there did not survive the charge of corrupt bargain between Adams and Clay that sent the first to the presidency and the second to the state department. Calhoun, having withdrawn from the presidential contest, won the vice-presidency.

Party Reorganization. The nationalist program of Adams did not ingratiate him with many Southerners, nor many Westerners for that matter. His cold, puritanical manner, his advocacy of a national university and astronomical observatory, larger appropriations for internal improvements, the Georgia Indian controversy that pitted state rights against nationalism, and the cry of corrupt bargain were factors that brought the Hero of New Orleans to the presidency in the next election. New, ill-defined parties were apparent during Adams' administration. The personal followings of Calhoun, Crawford, Benton, and Van Buren united with Jackson men to form the Democratic-Republican party. The Adams, Clay, and Webster groups coalesced to form the National Republican party. Both claimed lineal descent from the old Jeffersonian Republican party.

The Georgia Indian Controversy. One issue of the Adams period—the Georgia Indian controversy—merits emphasis. The president believed that the treaty of Indian Springs, negotiated toward the end of Monroe's administration, had been fraudulently manipulated. He therefore negotiated a new treaty with the Lower Creeks, postponing the date for removal of Indians from Georgia. Meanwhile, Governor George M. Troup ordered a survey of the lands preparatory to white settlement. In doing so, he defied central authority. Both Adams and Troup threatened the use of force, but a third treaty settled the controversy. In the interim, "the sovereign state of Georgia" established authority over all its area. Successful defiance of the central government encouraged South Carolinians in their tariff controversy with the United States.

The Tariff Issue. That controversy bespoke a changing economic base in politics. Calhoun as vice-president gave his casting vote against the Woolens Bill of 1827, thereby killing the tariff for that session of Congress. He explained the shift in his position in the interim since he enthusiastically supported the tariff of 1816. He then believed it was a policy that would unite the nation's sections; he was now convinced it was driving them apart. In the intervening years, it should be added, his South Carolina constituents had undergone transition. The plantation system and slavery were now firmly established in the Carolina upcountry, and a protective tariff that benefited the Northeast placed burdens upon the planter class.

Agricultural and Commercial Depression in the South. Much of the older South suffered from agricultural and commercial depression in the era from Jefferson to Jackson. Tidewater folk in particular found difficulty in adjusting themselves to an economy that promoted Northeastern industry and its concomitant, high finance. Virginia planters protested against distribution of wealth by legislative action. They preferred a national economy based on *laissez faire*. The depression along the South Atlantic seaboard was a factor that depleted the population as Southerners sought new homes in the West. A growing feeling in the South, and especially in South Carolina, that a policy of tariff protection benefited the manufacturing section and burdened the Southern region stimulated a spirit of protest. Depressed economy in the state and its commercial capital, Charleston, brought the central government's tariff policy into bold relief. The nullification controversy was hardly logic chopping, with the sole end a state rights interpretation of the Constitution. The crisis was intensified by the political break between Jackson and Calhoun which replaced the South Carolinian by Van Buren as the heir apparent to the presidency.

Nullification Doctrine. Calhoun's reply to the tariff of 1828 was the *South Carolina Exposition and Protest*, published anonymously by the legislature. It proposed state interposition as the rightful remedy, emulating the example of the Kentucky and Virginia Resolutions of thirty years before. The tariff of 1832, approved by a two-thirds majority in each house of Congress, was designed to make protection a permanent policy. Calhoun's answer was a more refined and polished statement of the doctrine of nullification than that embodied in the *Protest*. The "Fort Hill" letter of August 28, addressed to Governor James Hamilton, Jr., predicated his argument on the compact theory of the Union. The Constitution was a contract entered into by thirteen "principals" who were sovereign and free to accept or reject it. The Union was one, not of individuals, but of states, and they delegated limited powers to an "agent" who was not a party to the contract. It followed logically that a principal could protect itself against an act of Congress which it deemed unconstitutional by nullifying it in convention. The general government must acquiesce in this procedure, but it could propose any one of three solutions to the problem. It could abandon the power by repealing the obnoxious act, it could compromise the issue with the state, or it could propose a constitutional amendment, and if it were approved by three-fourths of the principals the questionable act became constitutional. If a state were still dissatisfied, it could as a last resort abandon the Union. Nullification was a means of preserving the Union; secession of destroying it. (*See Document No. 19.*)

Nullification in Practice. The South Carolina legislature acted promptly on the Calhoun procedure. It called a November convention which adopted an ordinance nullifying the tariff acts of 1828 and 1832. President Jackson used mild, persuasive language in his December message to Congress, reserving forceful, dynamic words for his Proclamation of December 10. "Disunion by armed force is *treason*," he asserted, and the duty of the executive was clear. Henry Clay, whom Jackson defeated for the presidency a few weeks before, was willing to sponsor a compromise tariff bill that provided for a gradual reduction of the schedules until they approached a revenue basis in 1842. Calhoun, who resigned the vice-presidency to succeed Hayne in the Senate, supported the bill; and it became law along with a companion measure, the "bloody" Force Bill, which authorized the use of force to collect revenue in South Carolina. An adjourned session of the convention then rescinded the November ordinance, but it adopted another, nullifying the Force Bill, which remained unrescinded. Both parties to the conflict could claim victory: Jackson—tariff duties had been collected uninterruptedly in Charleston; Calhoun—thanks to the steadfastness of his state, the protective principle had been abandoned. Other Southern states sympathized with South Carolina, though none approved nullification.

Origin of the Whig Party. The movement led by Calhoun was a contributing factor in the birth of the Whig party in 1834 and consolidation of Jackson men in the Democratic party. The Nullifiers, other state rights men alienated by Jackson's policies, Clay's National Republicans, and Anti-Masons united against King Andrew I as their Whig ancestors had revolted against the tyranny of King George III. Calhoun camped on the edge of the party until Jackson retired in 1837, and then he joined the Democratic fold. The new party, a conglomeration of diverse elements held together by opposition to Jacksonism, had no other reason for existence until Clay belatedly gave it a platform after the Whig victory of 1840. The party provided a substantial number of Southerners with a political home until its demise in the early 1850's. By that time a new issue, containment of slavery, or perhaps its abolition, received all-absorbing attention.

— 10 —

SLAVERY: CRITICS AND
DEFENDERS

European Search for a Labor Supply. It has been estimated that five million Africans crossed the Atlantic to the New World by the end of the eighteenth century. If this number approximates the truth, as many Negroes as whites participated in converting a raw hemisphere to the uses of mankind. From the arrival of Christopher Columbus on San Salvador, Europeans sought a source of labor supply for the menial tasks of subduing the wilderness that was America. The Great Explorer looked upon the Arawak with covetous eyes, and his successors, whether Spaniards, Portuguese, English, Dutch, or French, endeavored to convert Indians to forced labor. They met with only partial success. While Africans were hardly as docile as tradition represents them, they adjusted themselves to exploitation better than native Americans. By the seventeenth century their superior qualities as laborers were widely recognized.

Early Antislavery Sentiment in the South. How many consciences were disturbed over holding human beings in bondage, in early or later years of slavery, will never be known. Antislavery sentiments were expressed now and then in the colonial era, and some Revolutionary Fathers thought the time propitious to end an anomalous institution. Under the egalitarian spell of current philosophy, Northern states, where slaves were few and presented no great social or economic problem, provided emancipation, usually for the postnati. Delaware, Maryland, and Virginia also considered emanciptive measures, but no practical device seemed expedient. Nevertheless, in this early period there were frequent expres-

sions of antislavery sentiment in the South. Many slaveholders were potential abolitionists, and the growing
number of free Negroes attested their convictions on the
subject. Social reformer Jefferson, who embedded a
"free and equal" philosophy in the Declaration, pondered the problem in his *Notes on Virginia,* with colonization as a sequel to emancipation; and he inspired his
grandson, Thomas Jefferson Randolph, with antislavery
and gradual manumission views presented to the Virginia
legislature in 1832. (*See Document No. 20.*)

Cotton Production Perpetuates Slavery. Meanwhile, as we have seen, the introduction of cotton and
the invention of the gin gave slavery a more formidable
economic base. Slaves were as much a part of the westward movement as the whites who led them to new cotton, tobacco, and sugar frontiers, where they made contributions toward economic exploitation far beyond contemporary recognition. Foreign sources were closed
by 1808, but slaves brought forth progeny fully as fast
as their white neighbors to supply the increasing demand
for labor in new Southern commonwealths.

American Colonization Society. Everywhere, North
as well as South, free Negroes were regarded with misgivings. In four states of the Old South—Maryland, Virginia, North Carolina, and Kentucky—the right to vote
was withdrawn; and by 1821 only five Northern states
considered them worthy of the ballot. Colonization
seemed a happy solution to many Americans, and Bush-
rod Washington led men of moderate views in organiz-
ing the American Colonization Society in 1817. The
Society promoted emancipation, but it also contemplated removal of a racial minority from the limits of the
United States and provision of an opportunity in an
African environment where Negroes' "latent talent"
could be developed. The Society's success was so in-
finitesimal that it ran its course by the 1830's. The cost
of transportation to Liberia, reluctant support from a
limited number of sponsors, and lack of enthusiasm
among free Negroes for "return to the homeland" mili-
tated against success. After all, America was home; they
and members of their race still in bondage had made
tangible contributions in establishing it.

The "Positive Good" Theory. Before the 1820's Southerners had apologized for slavery, but in that decade a few of them began advancing a "positive good" theory, stirred in part by abolitionist criticism from the outside. Senator William Smith of South Carolina "justified slavery on the broadest principles, without qualification or reserve," and Thomas Cooper, transplanted Englishmen from the same state, pointed to historical and biblical precedents. And Stephen D. Miller, governor of South Carolina, characterized the institution as "a national benefit" rather than "a national evil."

Events of 1831 Focus Attention on Slavery. Three events of 1831 focused attention on the slavery controversy. In January William Lloyd Garrison began publication in Boston of the *Liberator* which advocated "immediate and uncompensated abolition." At the masthead of his paper he placed the challenging statement, "The compact which exists between the North and the South is a covenant with death and an agreement with hell." Such provocative preachments made his weekly paper, with a circulation that never exceeded 3,000, grist for Southern mills and created antagonists who publicized his incendiary attacks. In August of the same year Nat Turner's insurrection at Southampton, Virginia, in which sixty-one whites were massacred, underscored Southern fears of dreaded revolt. The next session of the legislature engaged in a long debate on the problem of slavery. Should the Old Dominion embark upon a plan of gradual manumission, or should it strengthen the slave code to prevent further uprisings? Younger delegates from the valley and the mountains—James McDowell, George W. Summers, Charles J. Faulkner—might deplore slavery's evils, view with alarm the Old Dominion's economic decline, commend advantages of a sturdy white yeomanry, and urge emancipation. Only nine votes from Tidewater and Piedmont joined with the western minority, and a plan of gradual manumission was rejected by a vote of 73 to 58. Opposition to slavery all but disappeared. And where Virginia led, other states followed. The hundred antislavery societies in the South in the 1820's nearly vanished by mid-century. With a few exceptions, persistent antislavery Southerners moved to the more congenial North.

The Antislavery Crusade in the 1830's. Although Garrisonian doctrine apparently had only limited influence, the antislavery movement reached large proportions in the 1830's. The crusade sought "moral reform" through "moral suasion." Particularly prominent were Congregational and Presbyterian clergymen, businessmen, college teachers, and members of professions. Lane Theological Seminary in Cincinnati became a hotbed of antislavery agitation. Theodore Dwight Weld, Charles G. Finney, and Henry B. Stanton stimulated the Western impulse. The Kentucky slaveholder, James G. Birney, moved north to participate in the movement, and so did the Grimké sisters of South Carolina, Sarah and Angelina, the younger of whom married Weld. Newspapers, schools, and churches served as agencies. Pamphlets were issued and petitions were sent to Congress and state legislatures. The American Anti-Slavery Society was born in 1833, and state and local societies flourished. The purpose of all this activity was to convince people that slavery was a sin (Dwight L. Dumond, ed., *Letters of James Gillespie Birney*, 1938, I, vii).

Political Antislavery, 1840-1860. By the end of the decade the movement became political. The Liberty party emerged in 1839, with Birney as its candidate for the presidency. Here was a man who had experienced slavery firsthand, for he had grown tobacco in his native Kentucky Bluegrass and cotton in northern Alabama with slave labor. Well educated at Transylvania and at the College of New Jersey, he had studied law at Philadelphia and served briefly in the Kentucky and Alabama legislatures. For a few years in the early thirties he became an agent for the American Colonization Society, but abandoned it as a forlorn hope. Freeing his own slaves, he endeavored to start an antislavery paper at Danville, but removed from that inhospitable community to Cincinnati to publish the *Philanthropist* in 1836. The following year he moved to New York to become executive secretary of the American Anti-Slavery Society. Seven thousand men deserted old parties to vote for him in 1840; over 60,000 supported him for the presidency four years later. As a protest group, the Liberty party was a harbinger of an idea that would with proper nourishment expand into a force to be reckoned with. Political antislavery gained momentum at midcentury with the appearance of the Free Soil party, dedicated to a policy of containment. That party in turn was absorbed by the Republicans in 1854, and they continued the battle for exclusion of the peculiar institution from the Western territories. Civil war would decide the issue—for the slaveholding states as well as frontier areas.

Dew and the Proslavery Argument. Meanwhile, Southerners had been weaving their defenses of slavery into a formal proslavery argument. The "positive good" theorists of the 1820's did not develop the concept into an elaborate statement of their position that lent itself readily to popular consumption. The first formal defense of slavery—Thomas R. Dew's *Review of the Debate in the Virginia Legislature of 1831 and 1832* —emanated from the Old Dominion's crisis following Nat Turner's insurrection. A graduate of William and Mary College in 1820, Dew became professor of history, metaphysics, and political law at his alma mater in 1826 and president of the college a decade later. His defense, first published at Richmond in 1832, was often reprinted before 1860. It served as a model for some of the other defenses that appeared in the interim.

Dew presented historical, biblical, economic, and social defenses of slavery. Calling upon the ancients as witnesses, he found recognition of slavery and inequality. He and other defenders, as well as abolitionists, read the Bible anew, seeking instances that would prove their contentions. From the Virginian's point of view, slavery was upheld by both Testaments, for the lawgiver Moses and the Apostle Paul sanctioned it. Surely white men of the South violated neither history nor scripture in enslaving inferior Africans. Economically, the institution was profitable. The sale of Virginia's surplus slaves to the Southwest yielded a return only slightly less than the profit from tobacco production. The government's tariff policy rather than the peculiar institution was responsible for the South's backwardness. Emancipation followed by

colonization would be impracticable: the process would
be expensive, the removal of a labor supply an economic
hardship upon planters, and adjustment to an African
environment difficult for freedmen. An insuperable social
problem would result from emancipation without colonization. The new philosophy repudiated Jefferson's concept expressed in the Declaration. Natural rights concepts disappeared; inequality became Southern ortho-
doxy. Slaves were society's mudsills.

Hammond's Defense. Other well-known Southerners, including the novelist William Gilmore Simms,
Chancellor William Harper, and Governor James H.
Hammond, all South Carolinians, advanced proslavery
arguments. In 1845 the last presented the usual defenses,
but in his economic approach he anticipated some of the
extremists' arguments of the 1850's. Hammond admitted
that, generally speaking, slave labor was more expensive
than free labor. Owners must provide food, clothing,
housing, and medical care in infancy and old age as well
as in productive years. The slave must be "well fed and
well clothed, if not for humanity's sake, that he may do
good work, retain health and life, and rear a family to
supply his place." Hammond would be willing to shift
from slave labor to free—if free labor were available
and if his slaves could be properly cared for in freedom.
But as no other labor was obtainable—at the pittance
Englishmen paid their workers—slaveholders must continue with their "dear labor, under the consoling reflection that what is lost to us, is gained to humanity."
Hammond was saying, in effect, that slaves had social
security vastly superior to that provided by English "poor
laws." (See Document No. 21.) He presented one side
of the case. To antislavery advocates, the whole proslavery argument seemed flimsy indeed.

The Position of the Slave. And what of the slave,
the person vitally involved in the torrent of polemics
that raged with increasing vituperation as the ante-
bellum era advanced?

Slavery in its least offensive administration: Kindly
masters and sympathetic mistresses. Abundance of plain
food, medical attention in periods of illness and accident.
(See Document No. 22.) Occasions for religious devo-

tion, Negro exhortations, sermons that emphasized obligations of servants to masters. Manumissions through special acts and wills. Frolics and spirituals, harvest and Christmas holidays, visits to other plantations. Encouraging words as compensation for productivity—of more cotton and more children. Opportunities to learn the white man's ways of life and methods of work. Sweet Saturday in the afternoon. Sunday lasts forever.

Slavery at its worst: Cruel Monday. Crude housing, monotonous diet. Long hours at hard labor. Simon Legrees, ignorant, overbearing overseers. Rough talk and obscene language. Lashings, beatings, whippingposts. Man without dignity. Honest toil and burden bearing without hope of graduation from servile status. Slave women put upon by white men. Separation of husbands and wives, parents and children, in the slave trade. Learning to read and write forbidden. Mental torture that accompanied lack of privilege and opportunity. An anomalous institution in an enlightened age. (*See Document No. 23.*)

History can never record with exactness the innermost feelings of slaves when they contemplated their inferior position, their hopelessness in a system that closed the door to personal independence and responsibility. Qualities of patience, forbearance, and toleration enabled many to adjust themselves without complete loss of happiness to the lowly station into which they were born and in which they were destined to continue. But there were sufficient expressions of protest to indicate resentment and dissatisfaction. Every absconding, every slave revolt, was tangible evidence of desperate effort to break the bonds of slavery. A few written records, by Negroes born in slavery or kidnapped into it, reveal the hard lot of an unprivileged class.

Slavery Agitation and the Churches. As the South turned from apology for slavery to its defense, churches shifted their attitudes toward human bondage. In the early years of the Republic, religious groups condemned the institution; later they followed the prevailing attitude. Well-known Southern clergymen—Benjamin H. Palmer, James H. Thornwell, Thornton Stringfellow, William A. Smith—promoted the doctrine of inequality in sermons and books, and contributed much of the data that found expression in the biblical defense of slavery. And when Northern members of religious bodies became critical of slaveholding ministers and missionaries, and sought to unfrock them, disruption followed. Two of the largest denominations—Methodists and Baptists—split in 1845, and the Methodist Episcopal Church, South, and the Southern Baptist Convention were formed. These two groups in particular appealed to Negroes, many of whom continued in their faith separately in the postwar period.

The Problem of Race. Southern rationalization of the peculiar institution that relegated the slave to a position of inferiority impressed many nonslaveholders who saw merit in the social discipline slavery afforded. The problem of race loomed larger as Negro population increased. The social problem in freedom seemed insoluble: How could Anglo-Saxons and "biologically inferior Negroes" live on terms of equality, especially in those areas in which Africans were a majority or a large minority? This insuperable problem provided a basis of strength not afforded by the economics of slavery. An unreasoned belief in a threat of social amalgamation gave slavery defenders a strong talking point as they pictured the challenge to racial purity.

— 11 —

SOUTHERN NATIONALISM

Manifest Destiny. Americans of the forties and fifties were convinced that territorial advancement to the westward was inevitable. Texas was annexed, California and the intervening territory were acquired, and the Oregon question was solved by extending the forty-ninth parallel to the Pacific. The Gadsden Purchase in 1853 rounded out the contiguous territory of the United States to its present limits. Southerners shared the American rage that characterized the "roaring forties." Expansionist dreams antedated the decade, however, for Southwesterners aided Texans in acquiring independence from Mexico in 1836, and many urged immediate annexation. While the "aggressive slaveocracy" was hardly conspiratorial, the prospect of an additional slaveholding state was undoubtedly an object. Westerners, whether north or south of the Ohio, gave enthusiastic support to the Mexican War. Acquisitions of the 1840's provided issues aplenty for the fifteen unfinished years of the ante-bellum period. The most serious divisive factor involved the question of slavery expansion into the new Western territory.

Slavery Extension as a Political Issue. Actually, there was no valid reason why slavery's expansion should have been a sectional political issue in the forties and fifties. In a notable essay Charles W. Ramsdell marshaled evidence to show that slavery had already reached its natural limits in East Texas, Arkansas, and Missouri. Climate and geography excluded the institution from territory west of that line except in parts of California, which had decided against slavery upon admission; and also from areas south of the border despite filibustering expeditions of the 1850's. Yet candidates for office, North and South, used containment and extension issues effectively in acquiring office or continuing therein. The clashing viewpoints involved "a theoretical Negro in an impossible place."

The Slavery Issue in 1848. Despite the gossamer cloth of the slavery expansion issue, it profoundly affected national political parties in the two decades under review. Whigs and Democrats were increasingly conscious of Northern and Southern wings. Lewis Cass's doctrine of squatter sovereignty, which would transfer the problem of slavery's extension from Congress to the territories, seemed a happy solution of the sectional ques-

tion in 1848, but did not win without a significant protest from the fire-eating William L. Yancey in the Alabama Platform, which demanded congressional protection of slavery in the Mexican Cession. But squatter
sovereignty prevailed, though its advocate lost by the nar-
rowest of majorities to the slaveholding hero of Buena
Vista, Zachary Taylor, whose enthusiasm for Whiggism
was certainly not pronounced. Prophetic in the campaign was the appearance of the Free Soil party, a combination of antislavery Democrats, Conscience Whigs,
and former Liberty party men, whose platform was
containment and whose slogan was "Free Soil, Free
Speech, Free Labor, and Free Men." Van Buren, its presidential candidate, polled three hundred thousand popular votes.

The Compromise of 1850. Taylor disappointed
Southerners who expected that he would pursue a vigorous policy for slavery's protection and expansion. He
favored admission of California with its irregularly
formed free-state constitution, and he also encouraged
inhabitants of New Mexico territory to inaugurate a
statehood movement. The disappointed presidential
aspirant, Henry Clay, who viewed the executive with a
jealous eye, advocated a solution of all sectional problems by a grandiose compromise. As finally constituted,
it proposed admission of California as a free state, prohibition of slave trade in the District of Columbia, a
stronger fugitive slave measure and organization of New
Mexico and Utah territories with postponement of
a decision on slavery until they framed state constitutions. The boundary dispute between New Mexico and
Texas was settled in favor of the territory's contention,
but the state would receive a ten-million dollar compensation. Giants of the past generation, the dying Calhoun and the aged Webster and Clay, made impressive
speeches, but their eloquent appeals changed no votes.
The astute leadership of Stephen A. Douglas and the
votes of more Democrats than Whigs brought Senate
approval of the five component measures.

Secession Movement of 1850. Growing tension
between the sections as the 1840's advanced led disturbed Southerners to calculate the value of the Union.

The half-dozen years at mid-century (1847-1852) witnessed a secession movement that reached a climax in the Nashville Convention. Delegates from Virginia and Tennessee and all of the deep South states except Louisiana assembled in June of 1850 to devise means of resisting Northern aggression. The convention adjourned to await the outcome of pending legislation before Congress. Favorable action on the compromise measures lessened influence of Southern extremists, and the November session attracted fewer delegates. The Nashville Convention demanded either recognition of the South's constitutional rights in the Western territory or division of it by extending the 36° 30′ line to the Pacific; and it reasserted the right of secession.

Southern State Conventions. Of far greater influence was the work of a Georgia Convention that assembled in December. Moderates, including Howell Cobb (Democrat), Robert Toombs, and Alexander H. Stephens (Whigs), controlled it and adopted a series of resolutions known as the Georgia Platform. Its "planks" endorsed compromise as a means of settling sectional disputes, pledged the state to abide by the Compromise of 1850 and to remain in the Union so long as it safeguarded "the rights and principles it had been designed to perpetuate," but warned that Georgia would resist, even to the Union's disruption, prohibition of slavery in New Mexico and Utah territories, its abolition in the District of Columbia, serious modification of the Fugitive Slave Act, or denial of statehood to a slaveholding territory. The last resolution underscored the rendition law: "it is the deliberate opinion of this Convention, that upon the faithful execution of the Fugitive Slave Bill depends the preservation of our much loved Union." (*See Document No. 24.*)

The Platform was both a promise and an ultimatum to the North. Its general acceptance over the South allayed secession sentiment and helped to avert a crisis. The Mississippi Convention of 1851 was also controlled by moderates, and its failure to adopt a secession ordinance made South Carolina action inopportune. Actually, extremists outnumbered moderates in that state's convention of 1852, but the minority defeated positive action by parading as coöperationists. South Carolina should not pursue a lone policy; it should await coöperation of other Southern states before embarking on a secession program.

"Finality" of the Compromise. The crisis had passed, but would. it return? National political parties were determined that the settlement should be permanent. The 1852 platforms of the Whig and Democratic parties declared that they accepted the compromise as a final solution of the slavery question. But the Free Soil party, or Free Democracy, declared otherwise, and many members of major parties had little faith in its permanency. Northern state legislatures had already passed personal liberty laws designed to thwart enforcement of the fugitive rendition act. Southern Whigs favored nomination of the incumbent Millard Fillmore, but the more numerous Northern branch of the party insisted on Winfield Scott. The conservative Franklin Pierce, Democratic "doughface" from New Hampshire, was chosen president by an overwhelming majority. Some Southern Whigs had already deserted the party, or would do so. Among them were the Georgians, Toombs and Stephens.

The Southern Rights Movement. There was little active interest in secession at mid-century outside of South Carolina and. Mississippi. The views of the extreme fire-eaters—Ruffin, Yancey, Rhett, and John A. Quitman—transcended public opinion. One of their number, Henry L. Benning of Georgia, even proposed an independent, unitary republic, for that type of government would restrain state rights and put slavery under control of its ardent defenders. Yet moderates felt little equanimity, and the atmosphere was not conducive to tranquillity: the good faith of the North remained a question mark. The crisis past, efforts to protect Southern rights and achieve greater security in the Union became desiderata. To this end the South resorted to commercial conventions and to search for constitutional guarantees.

The Effect of Contemporary Literature. Contemporary literature widened the gulf between North and South by convincing the one of its righteousness and the other of its rightness. Harriet Beecher Stowe's *Uncle*

Tom's Cabin (1852) did not cause the Civil War, as Lincoln quizzically implied, but it had tremendous effect in creating a state of mind. Uncle Tom's martyrdom, Little Eva's "spiritual beauty," the trials and tribulations of the absconding George and Eliza, Colonel Shelby's kindly benevolence, Simon Legree's villainy—these gave her book popular appeal. Despite defects as a novel, it was a best seller on both sides of the Atlantic. Southerners raged and fumed at misrepresentations, and some of them replied in forceful invective.

Hinton R. Helper, an antislavery North Carolinian, looked at slavery economically in his *Impending Crisis of the South* (1857). Using census reports of 1790 and 1850, he argued that whereas the Northern and Southern states were equal in the earlier period, the North had greatly outdistanced the South in the interim. The explanation: free labor in one section, slave labor in the other. He appealed to Southern nonslaveholders who, he thought, suffered most from the institution. (*See Document No. 25.*) He had no sympathy for the Negro, as his post-Civil War writings demonstrated. Again Southerners fretted (*see Document No. 26*); Northerners accepted his figures at face value and marveled that Southern men were unconvinced by one of their own number who "proved" the unprofitableness of slave labor.

No defender of slavery ever succeeded in writing a best seller, though Virginia's George Fitzhugh presented the fullest flowering of proslavery exaggeration. His first book, *Sociology for the South; or, The Failure of Free Society* (1854), compared free and slave society to the disparagement of the free. He contrasted the social security of the slave and the pitiable condition of factory workers in the free North and England. He closed his argument with an aggressive call to conflict: "For thirty years the South has been a field on which abolitionists, foreign and domestic, have carried on an offensive warfare. Let us now, in turn, act on the offensive, transfer the seat of war, and invade the enemy's territory." He did so in *Cannibals All! or, Slaves Without Masters* (1857). Free laborers were actually wage slaves; their lot would be improved if factory managers and mine operators converted their status to slavery and assumed responsibility for their welfare. The Southern system should be extended to the North and to Western Europe.

The Kansas-Nebraska Act.   Meanwhile, a political event undid the finality of the 1850 settlement. The Kansas-Nebraska Act of 1854 had far-reaching results. The territories of Kansas and Nebraska were organized on a popular sovereignty basis, and the act explicitly repealed the Missouri Compromise's Section 8, which excluded slavery from the Louisiana Purchase north of 36° 30′. That provision gave antislavery men, whether of the abolitionist or containment stripe, an opportunity to renew their warfare on the peculiar institution. And it gave Abraham Lincoln and many another politician an opportunity to rise from obscurity to prominence. The villainy of Stephen A. Douglas has gone the way of other myths; his sponsorship of the bill has been explained in terms of railroad interests and westward expansion. Southerners, too, have been absolved by historians of villainy in the piece. Copious evidence supports the view that the South's public figures and newspapers opposed the measure which would reopen the acrimonious debates of 1850, and finally endorsed it reluctantly as a test of the South's equal rights in the common property of the nation.

Bleeding Kansas and Its Aftermath.   The fact remains that the act of 1854 led to "bleeding" Kansas, which bled more profusely in Northern newspapers than on the territory's soil. And it also led to the birth of the Republican party, a sectional organization committed to free soil in the Western territories. The ruffianism of Southern migrants to Kansas was partly real and partly manufactured. The internal history of Kansas indicates that neither free-state men nor "border ruffians" had a monopoly on political virtue or lack of it, and that much of the border warfare concerned conflicting land claims rather than the slavery issue. The Dred Scott decision, which placed the Southern interpretation on popular sovereignty, and the Lecompton Constitution, which embodied subterfuge rather than a clear-cut vote on the slavery issue, inflamed the Northern mind. On the other hand, John Brown's raid on Harpers Ferry did even more to inflame the Southern mind. This act of violence, condemned by moderate Northerners, gave Southern extremists another opportunity to renew agitation for independence. Here was tangible evidence of their warnings: abolitionists would not stop short of fomenting servile insurrections. Meanwhile, Lincoln and Douglas debated the slavery issue on the prairies of Illinois as they sought election to the Senate in 1858. And Douglas explained, in his "Freeport Doctrine," that a hostile territorial legislature could exclude slavery by refusal to enact a slave code.

The Election of 1860. These events of the decade made the election of 1860 a genuine struggle for power, intraparty as well as interparty. As a political contest that might mean disruption or continuation of the Union, it was especially significant because it marked the demise of the last national party. The Whigs had disappeared by the middle of the decade, though a Southern remnant functioned as Know-Nothings or Americans in 1856. The Democratic party, certainly a bond of union, failed to survive its national convention at Charleston. Yancey led Southern members in insisting upon a platform of federal protection of slavery in the territories; Northern Democrats expressed willingness to abide by the Supreme Court's decision—with Douglas's "Freeport Doctrine" lurking in the background. When the Northern platform was adopted, lower South Democrats "seceded" from the convention. Two rival parties appeared with Douglas and John C. Breckinridge of Kentucky as their candidates. (*See Document No. 27.*) Both groups favored a Pacific railroad and acquisition of Cuba. Some Southern moderates, former Whig-Americans, united in support of John Bell of Tennessee in the Constitutional Union party, whose brief platitudinous platform demanded the Constitution as it was and the Union as it is.

Republicans experienced little difficulty in framing a platform advocating the Wilmot Proviso principle—nonextension of slavery into the federal territories—a transcontinental railroad, a homestead act, and a protective tariff. The preconvention favorite, William H. Seward, was shelved in favor of Abraham Lincoln, whose relative obscurity, Western democracy, and simple honesty made him more available than the New Yorker whose name was inseparably associated with "irrepressible conflict" and Eastern radicalism.

The election of 1860 was really two elections. When Northern voters went to the polls, the choice was between Lincoln and congressional prohibition of slavery in the territories, or Douglas and popular sovereignty, which would permit voters to determine, in and for the territorial period, the issue of slavery. Southerners chose either Breckinridge and congressional protection of slavery in the territories or Bell and the more noncommittal preservation of the Union under the Constitution. A "Black Republican" president was chosen. Southerners had been saying for some time that such an eventuality would lead to secession.

Why the War Came.   The election of a Republican president was not so much a cause of secession as it was a culmination of a generation's divergent thought and culture. Elder statesmen of 1860 could remember the days of their youth when American nationality dominated the thinking of public forums; when sectional issues were the exception rather than the rule; when political parties united men without reference to regional nativity or local attachment. Three decades of controversy provoked questions, then convictions, concerning the colonial position of a minority section and the expediency of its continuation in the Union.

Outwardly, at least, Southerners placed their faith in the Constitution, a contractual agreement among the states. It delegated limited authority to the general government, reserving all other powers to the states, and it recognized slavery. With the organic act Southerners had little quarrel. In attacking slavery and in using implied and derived powers, the central agent, dominated by King Numbers, violated the contract. Increasingly, Northerners were talking about a higher law than the Constitution, a moral law that sanctioned disregard for the sacred compact.

Writers have spilled much ink on the causes of the war, or at least on events and personality clashes that explain its coming. The Beards spoke of an economic-political rivalry, "a social cataclysm in which the capitalists, laborers, and farmers of the North and West drove from power in the national government the planting aristocracy of the South." James Ford Rhodes believed that Southern insistence on maintaining and expanding slavery—"an unrighteous cause"—led to secession and war, though he generously absolved slaveholders from responsibility, for the Northeast had contributed toward fastening the institution on the South. Phillips pointed to the problem of race and the maintenance of white supremacy. Allan Nevins combined two themes into one as the conflict's "main root": "the problem of slavery *with its complementary problem of race-adjustment.*" The tragedy's principal source "was the refusal of either section to face these conjoined problems squarely and pay the heavy costs of a peaceful settlement." And Avery Craven, who wrote not of causes but of the "coming," found a psychological base, a set of symbols. Southerners conjured up in their minds a Northern stereotype: fanatics who would go to any lengths to destroy Southern civilization. Northerners thought of all Southerners as fire-eating extremists who would destroy the Union to perpetuate an evil that kept human beings in bondage and disgraced the principles on which the Republic was founded. It was a conflict of " 'right' versus 'rights' that placed issues beyond the democratic process and rendered the great masses of men, North and South, helpless before the drift into war."

A Southerner of an earlier generation deserves a final word on a problem that defies definitive solution. In 1902 a Harvard-educated Alabamian, William Garrott Brown, stated the challenge that faced Southerners in the years between 1830 and 1860: "It was the belated concern of the Northern mind about the things of the spirit, not its absorption in material enterprises, that boded ill to the plantation system. It was the North's moral awakening, and not its industrial alertness, its free thought, and not its free labor, which the Southern planter had to fear. The New England factory made no threat, the town meeting did. The Northwestern wheat farms and pork packeries and railways were harmless; but Oberlin College and Lovejoy's printing press and the underground railway were different. . . . The true danger from without was in the moral and intellectual forces which were at once the cause and the result of the North's progress" (*The Lower South in American History*, 1902, p. 88). Brown's words are worth pondering in an age when a minglement of minds yields an ever-expanding literature on the Civil War, its causes, and its consequences.

Part Two—DOCUMENTS

— Document No. 1 —

OPENING SESSION OF VIRGINIA'S HOUSE OF BURGESSES, JULY 30, 1619[1]

No "journals" of the House of Burgesses in its early years have been preserved. The following account of the opening session is a report compiled by John Pory, the assembly's speaker and the colony's secretary. The original was forwarded to London Company authorities in England and preserved in the British Public Record Office. The word "burgess" in this period means a voter or citizen in one of Virginia's "borroughs." Later it became synonymous with a representative in the general assembly's elective branch.

✓   ✓   ✓

The most convenient place we could finde to sitt in was the Quire of the Churche, Where Sir *George Yeardley* the Governour being sett downe in his accustomed place, those of the Counsel of Estate sate nexte him on both handes excepte onely the Secretary then appointed Speaker, who sate right before him; *John Twine* clerke of the General Assembly being placed nexte the Speaker and *Thomas Pierse* the Sergeant standing at the barre, to be ready for any service the Assembly should command him. But for as muche as mens affaires doe little

[1] H. R. McIlwaine, ed., *Journals of the House of Burgesses of Virginia, 1619-1658/59* (Richmond, 1915), pp. 4-6. Reprinted by permission of the Virginia State Library, Richmond.

prosper where Gods service is neglected; all the Burgesses took their places in the Quire, till a Prayer was said by Mr *Bucke,* the Minister, that it would please God to guide us and sanctifie all our proceedings to his owne glory, and the good of this Plantation, Prayer being ended, to the intente that as wee had begun at God Almighty soe wee might proceed with awful and due respecte towards his Lieutenant, our most gratious and dread Soveraigne, all the Burgesses were intreated to retyre themselves into the body of the Churche; which being done, before they were fully admitted, they were called in order and by name, and so every man (none staggering at it) tooke the oathe of Supremacy, and then entered the Assembly, At Captaine *Warde* the Speaker tooke exception, as at one that without any Commission or authority, had seatted himselfe either upon the Companies, and then his Plantation could not be lawfull, or on Captaine *Martins* Lande, and so he was but a limbe or member of him, and so there could be but two Burgesses for all. So Captaine *Warde* was commanded to absente himselfe, till such time as the Assembly had agreed what was fitt for him to doe. After muche debate they resolved on this order following,

> An order concluded by the General Assembly concerning Captaine *Warde July* 30th 1619 at the opening of the said Assembly.

At the reading of the names of the Burgesses Exception was taken against Captaine *Warde* as having planted here in *Virginia,* without any authority or commission from the Treasurer Counsell and Company in *Englande,* But considering he had bene at so great chardge and paines to augmente this Colony, and had adventured his owne person in the action, and since that time had brought home a goode quantity of fishe to relieve the Colony by waye of trade; and above all, because the Comission for authorising the General Assembly admitteth of two Burgesses out of every plantation with out restrainte or exception, Upon all these considerations the Assembly was contended to admitt of him and his Lieutenant (as members of their body and Burgesses into their society, provided that the said Captaine *Warde,* with all expeidition, that is to saye, between this and the nexte genera[1] Assembly (all lawful impediments excepted) should procure from the Tresurer and Counsell and Company in *Englande* a commission lawfully to establishe and plant himselfe and his Company, as the Chiefes of other Plantations have done, And in case he doe neglect this, he is to stande to the censure of the nexte Generall Assembly. To this Captaine *Warde,* in the presence of us all, having given his consente, and undertaken to performe the same, was together with his Lieutenant, by the voices of the whole Assembly first admitted to take the oath of Supremacy and then to make up their number, and to sitt amongst them.

This being done, the Governour himselfe alledged that before we proceeded any further, it behooved us to examine, whither it were fitt, that Captaine *Martins* Burgesses shoulde have any place in the Assembly, for as muche as he hath a clause in his Patente which doth not onely exempte him from that quality and uniformity of Lawes and orders, which the great charter saith, are to extende over the whole Colony, but also from diverse suche lawes as we must be enforced to make in the general Assembly. . . .

Upon the Motion of the Governour, discussed the same time in the Assembly, ensued this order following

    An Order of the General Assembly touching a   clause in Captaine *Martins* Patente at *James*   *Citty July* 30, 1619

After all the Burgesses had taken the oath of supremacy, and were admitted into the House, and all sett downe in their places, a copie of Captaine *Martins* Patente was produced by the Governour out of a Clause whereof it appeared, that when the general Assembly had made some kinde of lawes requisite for the whole Colony, he and his Burgesses and people might deride the whole company and chuse whether they would obey the same or no It was therefore ordered in Courte, that the foresaid two Burgesses should withdrawe themselves out of the Assembly till such time as Captaine *Martin* had made his personall appearance before them. . . .

Then came in a complainte against Captaine *Martin*

that having sente his Shallop to trade for corne into
the baye under the commaunde of Ensigne *Harrison,*
the saide Ensigne shoulde affirme to one *Thomas Davis,*
of *Paspaheighs,* Gent (as the said *Thomas Davis* deposed
upon oathe) that they had made a harde voiage, had
they not mett with a Canoa coming out of a creeke,
where their Shallop could not goe, For the Indians refusing to sell their Corne, those of the shallop entered
the Canoa with their armes and tooke it by force, measuring out the corne with a baskett they had, into the
shallop and (as the said Ensigne *Harrison* saith) given
them satisfaction in Copper, Beades, and other trucking
Stuffe, Hitherto Mr. *Davys* upon his oath. . . .

Upon this a letter or warrant was drawen in the name
of the whole Assembly to summon Captaine *Martin* to
appeare before them in forme following:

> By the Governour and general Assembly of *Vir-
> ginia.*

Captaine *Martine,* we are to request you upon sight
hereof, with all convenient speed to repaire hither to
James Citty, to treate and conferre with us about some
matters of espiciale importance, which concerne both
us, and the whole Colony, and your selfe, And of this we
pray you not to faile,

> *James Citty, July* 30th 1619.
> To our very loving friend Captaine *John Martin*
> Esquire, Master of the Ordinance.

These obstacles removed, the Speaker, who a long
time had bene extreame sickly, and therefore not able to
passe through long harangues, delivered in briefe to the
whole assembly the occasions of their meeting, Which
done, he read unto them the commission for establishing the Counsell of Estate and the Generall Assembly,
wherein their duties were described to the life,

Having thus prepared them, he read over unto them
the greate Charter or commission of priviledges, orders
and lawes sente by Sir *George Yeardly* out of *Englande*
which for the more ease of the Committees, having divided into fower books, he read the former two the same

forenoon, for expeditions sake, a second time over, and so they were referred to the perusall of twoe Committees, which did reciprocally consider of either, and accordingly brought in their opinions, But some man may here objecte to what ende we shoulde presume to refferre that to the examination of Committees, which the Counsell and Company in *Englande* had already resolved to be perfect and did expecte nothinge but our assente there unto. To this we answere, that we did it not to the ende to correcte or controll any thing therein contained, but onely in case we should finde ought not perfectly squaring with the state of this Colony, or any lawe which did presse or binde too harde, that wee might by waye of humble petition seeke to have it redressed; especially because this great Charter is to binde us and our heyers for ever. . . .

After dinner the Governor and those that were not of the Committees sate a seconde time, while the said Committees were employed in the perusall of those twoe bookes. And whereas the Speaker had propounded fower severall objects for the Assembly to consider on namely first, the great charter of orders, lawes and priviledges, Secondly which of the instructions given by the Counsell in *England* to my Lord *le Warre,* Captaine *Argall* or Sir *George Yeardley,* might conveniently putt on the habite of Lawes; Thirdly what Lawes might issue out of the private conceipte of any of the Burgesses, or any other of the Colony; and lastly what petitions were fitt to be sente home for *Englande* It pleased the Governor for expeditions sake to have the second objecte of the fower to be examined and prepared by himselfe and the non Committee. Wherein after having spente some three houres conference, the twoe Committees brought in their opinions concerning the twoe former bookes (the second of which beginneth at these wordes of the Charter.) And forasmuche as our intente is to establish one equall and uniforme kinde of government over all *Virginia* etc) which the whole Assembly, because it was late deferred to treatt of till the next morning.

— Document No. 2 —

NORTH CAROLINA'S BEEF, PORK, AND PELTRY TRADE [2]

Johann David Schoepf, a young German physician trained in botany, mineralogy, and forestry as well as in medicine, came to the United States in 1777 as "chief surgeon to the Ansbach troops." After the Revolution he toured the country, 1783-1784, from New Jersey south to East Florida, motivated by "curiosity" and a desire to collect "natural products." His account of deer, cattle, and hogs in North Carolina, and incidentally of the presence of bison in the back country, is a significant segment of his travel legacy.

✓   ✓   ✓

Most of the North American indigenous wild animals are still to be found in these extensive and thinly settled woods of the fore-country of North Carolina. Wolves, bears, wild cats, the brown tyger or cuguar, as well as the bison and the original, are often met with in North and South Carolina even far to the east of the mountains. . . . The Virginia deer . . . still ranges in these parts in large herds. Now and again we saw many of them pasturing together quite unconcerned. Their size is a little less than that of our fallow deer. . . . The export of their skins is a considerable item yearly in this province. A proof of the number of these animals is that one man on the New river has been able to shoot 175 head since the spring of this year, and simply for their pelts. If one cannot or will not shoot for himself, the game may be bought commonly for one or at most two

[2] Johann David Schoepf, *Travels in the Confederation* [1783-1784], trans. and ed. by Alfred J. Morrison (2 vols.; Philadelphia, 1911), II, 107-111.

Spanish dollars the head, which always gives more than a hundredweight of venison.

With the most careless handling domestic cattle have increased with the greatest rapidity. It is nothing uncommon for one man to own 100 or more head of horned cattle; some count their herds by the thousand, all running loose in the woods and swamps. By penning up the calves, and throwing out a little corn every day to the dams, the milch cows have been accustomed to come up to the dwelling-house from time to time to be milked. For each farm, the black cattle, sheep, and hogs are distinguished by special earmarks; horses are branded. Each planter's own peculiar mark is registered by law, and is thus a legitimate proof of ownership, and extinguishment or falsification of these marks is treated as felony. There is little beef salted for export; what is salted is said not to keep well, and to grow hard and lank. In general, the beef is of no especial goodness in any of the provinces south of Pensylvania and Maryland; the cattle themselves small and thin. But live cattle are exported to the West Indies from the coast country, and large herds are driven up from the farther regions to Pensylvania, and there fed for the Philadelphia market. Out of the woods and thin as they are, one head with another is sold to the cattle-handlers at 3 to 6 Spanish dollars; and to the owner, who has been at so little trouble and expence, this is almost clear gain. Their hogs likewise range throughout the year in the woods. Towards the coast in the pine forests, the cones of the pitch-pine, larger than those of the other sorts, are their favorite food. . . . Farther up the country the hogs find better mast beneath the numerous oaks, chestnuts, beech-trees, and chinquapins. In winter the sows make themselves beds of pine-twigs where they litter; the owner seeks them out, brings them in nearer the house, gives them a better bed of straw, and marks the pigs. Later, to accustom them to the plantation, they are called up several times a day and fed on corn stalks. In the autumn, after the maize-harvest, a number of hogs are brought in from the woods and placed on feed. A bushel of corn a week is allowed each head, for 5-6 weeks. The amount of corn made determines the number of hogs to be fed. Fattened hogs reach 3 to 500 pounds' weight. Live hogs sell at 3-3½ Spanish dollars the hundred. Nowhere on the whole continent is the breeding of swine so considerable or so profitable as in North Carolina. Besides what is consumed in the country, salted, exported, and lost in the woods, there are annually 10-12000 head driven to South Carolina or to Virginia. The North Carolinians therefore should not look a-skance, if their neighbors rally them for being pork-makers, for when the talk gets on their swine-breeding they themselves use the expression, 'We make pork.' But in these circumstances, a hog costing them next to nothing except for what goes into the fattening, the North Carolinians can send their salted hog-meat to market at a third or a half cheaper than their neighbors in the northern states where harder winters and more restricted pasturage makes the maintenance dearer. . . .

Such a quantity of neat cattle, horses, and hogs ranging about in the woods, many get from under the eye of the owners, are either not marked, or run off and are chased by predatory beasts into regions where the marks are not known, or multiply in unsettled parts of the country. All such cattle are called wild, and are no man's property except his on whose land they are found. But in certain parts there is a 'woods-right' so called, according to which every plantation has a fixed share of all wild herds thereabouts; and this right, like any other property, can be transferred or sold at will. Their hogs are especially apt to grow wild, not answering calls and difficult to bring tame again. . . .

— Document No. 3 —

CAROLINA BACK COUNTRY IN THE 1760'S[3]

A significant and revealing account of the Carolina Back Country was recorded by Charles Woodmason, English-born Anglican itinerant, who began his ministrations in 1766 and continued them for a half-dozen years. In this primitive world Woodmason witnessed the effect of the frontier upon the inhabitants, political and religious strife, and the emergence of small farms from the wilderness. In the following paragraphs he is concerned with religious matters, including the "evil" influences of New Light Baptists and Presbyterians.

ϟ   ϟ   ϟ

There is one Circumstance which I cannot but this publickly take Notice off and reprove, because it not only occasions the Non-observance of the Sabbath but is an Evil in it Self, and scandalous to the Country—and that is—The transacting of all Public Business on Saturdays. Thus We see Magistrates have their Sittings—Militia Officers their Musters—Merchants their Vendues—Planters their Sales, all on Saturdays: Is there any Shooting, Dancing, Revelling, Drinking Matches carrying on? It is all begun on Saturday, and as all these Meetings and Transactions are executed at Taverns, Not a Saturday in the Year, but some one or other of them (and at more than one Tavern) are statedly repeatedly carried on—So that at these Rendezvous there is more

[3] Richard J. Hooker, ed., *The Carolina Backcountry on the Eve of the Revolution: The Journal and Other Writings of Charles Woodmason, Anglican Itinerant* (Chapel Hill, 1953), pp. 96-100. Reprinted by permission of the University of North Carolina Press, Chapel Hill.

Company of a Saturday, than in the Church on Sunday:
And these Assemblies are not only carried on under Eye
of the Magistrates, but even by them—Most of them
being Store or Tavern Keepers. Thus Vice and Wicked-
ness is countenanc'd by those whose Duty it is to suppress
it—but their Interest to promote it. And yet several of
these Magistrates are Heads of these New Congregations:
. . . And herefrom arises the Evil of so few assembling
here at Divine Service ev'ry Lords Day: Saturday being chosen as a day whereon they may fully indulge
themselves in Drink, and so sleep it off on Sunday, to be
fit to attend Business on Monday, and so not two days
lost to them in the Week. . . .

It may be reply'd to me, That altho' People do stay at
home, and not come to Chapel on those Sundays when
there is no Sermon at the Meeting Yet that they employ
themselves in Religious Exercises, and Works of Edifica-
tion: What Works?—In Singing of Hymns and Spiritual
Songs—whereby their Hearts are greatly inflam'd with
Divine Love and Heav'nly Joy, and makes the H[oly]
G[host] be shed abroad in their Hearts. This is very fine
Talking: I could wish that all the *Doings* too, were equally
Innocent. But let me say, that these Assemblies at Pri-
vate Houses for Singing Hymns, is very reprehensible.
First because People may assemble in this Place, and
Sing, and then no Scandal would arise, and 2dly The
Hymns commonly sung, had far better be thrown into
the Fire. . . .

The best Things are most liable to Abuse—And
these Singing Matches lie under the Imputation of being
only Rendezvous of Idlers, under the Mask of Devotion.
Meetings for Young Persons to carry on Intrigues and
Amours. For all Classes of Villains, and the Vicious of
both Sexes to make Assignations; and for others to indulge themselves in Acts of Intemperance and Wantoness, So that these Religious Societies are Evil spoken off,
and therefore ought to be abolished. . . .

But let us go on, and examine if in the General Cor-
ruption of Manners these New Lights have made any
Reform in the Vice of Drunkenness? Truly, I wot not.
There is not one Hogshead of Liquor less consum'd since
their visiting us, or any Tavern shut up—So far from it,

that there has been Great Increase of Both. Go to any Common Muster or Vendue, Will you not see the same Fighting, Brawling Gouging, Quarreling as ever? And this too among the Holy ones of our New Israel? Are Riots, Frolics, Races, Games, Cards, Dice, Dances, less frequent now than formerly? Are fewer persons to be seen in Taverns? or reeling or drunk on the Roads? And have any of the Godly Storekeepers given up their Licences, or refus'd to retail Poison? If this can be made appear, I will yield the Point. . . .

The horrid Vice of Swearing has long been a reproach to the Back Inhabitants, and very justly—for few Countries on Earth can equal these Parts as to this grievous Sin. But has it ceas'd since the Admission of rambling Fanatics among us? I grant that it has with and among many, whom they have gain'd to their Sect. Yet still it too much prevails. But the Enormity of this Vice, when at the Highest, produc'd no Evils, Jarrs, disturbances Strifes, Contentions, Variance, Dissimulations, Envyings, Slanders, Backbitings and a thousand other Evils that now disturb both the Public Places and repose of Individuals. So that where they have cast out one Devil, Seven, and twice Seven others have enter'd In and possess the Man. For never was so much Lying, Calumny, Defamation, and all hellish Evils and vexations of this Sort that can spring from the Devil and his Angels, so brief so prevalent, so abounding as since the Arrival of these villanous Teachers, Who blast, blacken, Ruin, and destroy the Characters, Reputations, Credit and Fame of all Persons not linked with them to the Ruin of Society, the Peace of families, and the Settlement of the Country.

We will further enquire, if Lascivousness, or Wantoness, Adultery or Fornication [are] less common than formerly, before the Arrival of these *Holy* Persons? Are there fewer Bastards born? Are more Girls with their Virginity about them, Married, than were heretofore? The Parish Register will prove the Contrary: There are rather more Bastards, more Mullatoes born than before. Nor out of 100 Young Women that I marry in a Year have I seen, or is there seen, Six but what are with Child? And this as Common with the Germans on other Side the River, as among You on this Side: So that a

Minister is accounted as a Scandalous Person for even coming here to marry such People, and for baptizing their Bastard Children as the Law obliges Me to register All Parties who are Married, and all Children Born. This occasions such Numbers (especially of the Saints) to fly into the next Province, and up to the German Ministers and any where to get Married, to prevent their being register'd, as therefrom the Birth of their Children would be trac'd: And as for Adulteries, the present State of most Persons around 9/10 of whom now labour under a filthy Distemper (as is well known to all) puts that Matter out of all Dispute and shews that the Saints however outwardly Precise and Reserved are not one Whit more Chaste than formerly, and possibly are more privately Vicious.

And nothing more leads to this Than what they call their Love Feasts and Kiss of Charity. To which Feasts, celebrated at Night, much Liquor is privately carried, and deposited on the Roads, and in Bye Paths and Places. The Assignations made on Sundays at the Singing Clubs, are here realized. And it is no wonder that Things are as they are, when many Young Persons have 3. 4. 5. 6 Miles to walk home in the dark Night, with Convoy, thro' the Woods? Or staying perhaps all Night at some Cabbin (as on Sunday Nights) and sleeping together either doubly or promiscuously? Or a Girl being mounted behind a Person to be carried home, or any wheres. All this indeed contributes to multiply Subjects for the King in this frontier Country, and so is wink'd at by the Magistracy and Parochial Officers but at same time, gives great Occasion to the Enemies of Virtue, to triumph, for Religion to be scandalized and brought into Contempt; For all Devotion to be Ridicul'd, and in the Sequel, will prove the Entire banishment and End of all Religion—Confusion —Anarchy and ev'ry Evil Work will be the Consequence of such Lewdness and Immorality.

— Document No. 4 —

A PRINCETON TUTOR IN A VIRGINIA FAMILY 1773-1774 [4]

Philip Vickers Fithian, graduate of the College of New Jersey, served during the year 1773-1774 as tutor to the children of Robert Carter, master of "Nomini Hall" plantation in Virginia. His experiences in the Old Dominion were recorded in an informative journal and in sundry letters. The first of the paragraphs here quoted is extracted from a letter of December 1, 1773; the others are from the journal entry for January 4, 1774.

✦   ✦   ✦

I set out from home on the 20th of Octr and arrived at the Hon: Robert Carters, of Nominy, in Westmorland County, the 28th I began to teach his children the first of November. He has two sons, and one Nephew; the oldest Son is turned of seventeen, and is reading Salust and the greek grammer; the others are about fourteen, and in english grammer, and Arithmetic. He has besides five daughters which I am to teach english, the eldest is turned of fifteen, and is reading the spectator; she is employed two days in every week in learning to play the Forte-Piana, and Harpsicord—The others are smaller, and learning to read and spell. Mr Carter is one of the Councellors in the general court at Williamsburg, and possest of as great, perhaps the clearest fortune according to the estimation of people here, of any man in Vir-

[4] Fithian, Philip Vickers, *Journal and Letters of Philip Vickers Fithian, 1773-1774*, edited by Hunter Dickinson Farish. Williamsburg, 1957. By permission of Colonial Williamsburg, Inc. Pp. 26, 48-49.

ginia: He seems to be a good scholar, even in classical learning, and is remarkable one in english grammar; and notwithstanding his rank, which in general seems to countenance indulgence to children, both himself and Mrs Carter have a manner of instructing and dealing with children far superior, I may say it with confidence, to any I have ever seen, in any place, or in any family. . . . Mr. Carter has an over-grown library of Books of which he allows me the free use. It consists of a general collection of law books, all the Latin and Greek Classicks, vast number of Books on Divinity chiefly by writers who are of the established Religion; he has the works of almost all the late famous writers, as Locke, Addison, Young, Pope, Swift, Dryden, &c. in Short, Sir, to speak moderately, he has more than eight times your number. . . .

Mrs *Carter* is prudent, always cheerful, never without Something pleasant, a remarkable Economist, perfectly acquainted (in my Opinion) with the good-management of Children, intirely free from all foolish and unnecessary fondness. . . . Ben, the eldest, is a youth of genius: of a warm impetuous Disposition; desirous of acquiring Knowledge, docile, vastly inquisitive & curious in mercantile, and mechanical Matters, is very fond of Horsses, and takes great pleasure in exercising them— Bob, the other Brother, is By no means destitute of capacity, As Mr Marshal who was his last Tutor has asserted, & as many now suppose: He is extremely volatile & unsettled in his temper, which makes it almost wholly impossible to fix him for any time to the same thing—On which account he has made but very little advancement in any one Branch of Study, and this is attributed to Barrenness of Genius—He is slovenly, clumsy, very fond of Shooting, of Dogs, of Horses, But a very stiff untoward *Rider,* good natur'd, pleased with the Society of persons much below his Family, and Estate, and tho' quick and wrathful in his temper, yet he is soon moderated, & easily subdued—Harry the Nephew, is rather stoical, sullen, or saturnine in his make. He is obstinate, tho' Steady, and makes a slow uniform advance in his Learning, he is vastly kind to me, but in particular to my Horse, of his health or Indisposition—Miss *Priscilla,* the eldest Daughter about 16, is steady, studious, docile, quick of apprehension, and makes good progress in what She undertakes; If I could with propriety continue in the Family, I should require no stronger Inducement then the Satisfaction I should receive by seeing this young Lady become perfectly acquainted with any thing I propose so soon as I communicate it to her, but the situation of my affairs makes it out of my power to stay longer than a year; She is small of her age, has a mild winning Presence, a sweet obliging Temper, never swears, which is here a distinguished virtue, dances finely, plays well on key'd Instruments, and is upon the whole in the first Class of the female Sex.

Nancy the Second, is not without some few of those qualities which are by some (I think with great ill nature, and with little or no truth) said to belong intirely to the fair Sex. I mean great curiosity, Eagerness for superiority, Ardor in friend ship, But bitterness and rage where there is enmity—She is not constant in her disposition, nor diligent nor attentive to her business—But She has her excellencies, She is cheerful, tender in her Temper, easily managed by perswasion & is never without what seems to have been a common Gift of Heaven, to the *fair-Sex*, the *"Copia Verborum,"* or readiness of Expression!—She is only beginning to play the *Guitar,* She understands the Notes well, & is a graceful Dancer.

Fanny next, is in her Person, according to my Judgment, the Flower in the Family—She has a strong resemblance of her *Mama* who is an elegant, beautiful Woman—Miss Fanny seems to have a remarkable Sedateness, & simplicity in her countenance, which is always rather chearful than melancholy; She has nothing with which we can find Fault in her Person, but has something in the Features of her Face which insensibly pleases us, & always when She is in Sight draws our Attention, & much the more because there seems to be for every agreeable Feature a correspondent Action which improves & adorns it. Betsy next is young, quiet, and obedient—Harriot is bold, fearless, noisy and lawless; always merry, almost never displeased; She seems to have a Heart easily moved by the force of Music; She has learned many Tunes & can strike any Note, or Suc-

cession of Notes perfectly with the Flute or Harpsichord,
and is never wearied with the sound of Music either vocal
or *Instrumental.*

— Document No. 5 —

VIRGINIA BILL OF RIGHTS, 1776 [5]

*George Mason, one of the ablest constitutionalists of
the Revolutionary generation, drafted the Virginia Bill
of Rights. Some of its language was used by Jefferson in
the philosophic phrases of the Declaration of Independence;
and many of the concepts embodied in the first ten
amendments to the Constitution—the nation's Bill of
Rights—were earlier written into the Virginia document.*

✓   ✓   ✓

*A declaration of rights made by the representatives
of the good people of Virginia, assembled in full
and free convention; which rights do pertain to
them and their posterity, as the basis and foundation
of government.*

SECTION 1. That all men are by nature equally free
and independent, and have certain inherent rights, of
which, when they enter into a state of society, they cannot,
by any compact, deprive or divest their posterity;
namely, the enjoyment of life and liberty, with the means

[5] Ben: Perley Poore, comp., *The Federal and State Constitutions,
Colonial Charters, and Other Organic Laws
of the United States* (2 pts., 2nd ed.; Washington, 1878),
II, 1908-1909.

of acquiring and possessing property, and pursuing and obtaining happiness and safety.

SEC. 2. That all power is vested in, and consequently derived from, the people; that magistrates are their trustees and servants, and at all times amenable to them.

SEC. 3. That government is, or ought to be, instituted for the common benefit, protection, and security of the people, nation, or community; of all the various modes and forms of government, that is best which is capable of producing the greatest degree of happiness and safety, and is most effectually secured against the danger of maladministration; and that, when any government shall be found inadequate or contrary to these purposes, a majority of the community hath an indubitable, inalienable, and indefeasible right to reform, alter, or abolish it, in such manner as shall be judged most conducive to the public weal.

SEC. 4. That no man, or set of men, are entitled to exclusive or separate emoluments or privileges from the community, but in consideration of public services; which, not being descendible, neither ought the offices of magistrate, legislator, or judge to be hereditary.

SEC. 5. That the legislative and executive powers of the State should be separate and distinct from the judiciary; and that the members of the two first may be restrained from oppression, by feeling and participating the burdens of the people, they should, at fixed periods, be reduced to private station, return into that body from which they were originally taken, and the vacancies be supplied by frequent, certain, and regular elections, in which all, or any part of the former members, to be again eligible, or ineligible, as the laws shall direct.

SEC. 6. That elections of members to serve as representatives of the people, in assembly, ought to be free; and that all men, having sufficient evidence of permanent common interest with, and attachment to, the community, have the right of suffrage, and cannot be taxed or deprived of their property for public uses, without their own consent, or that of their representatives so elected, nor bound by any law to which they have not, in like manner, assented, for the public good.

SEC. 7. That all power of suspending laws, or the execution of laws, by any authority, without consent of the representatives of the people, is injurious to their rights, and ought not to be exercised.

SEC. 8. That in all capital or criminal prosecutions a man hath a right to demand the cause and nature of his accusation, to be confronted with the accusers and witnesses, to call for evidence in his favor, and to a speedy trial by an impartial jury of twelve men of his vicinage, without whose unanimous consent he cannot be found guilty; nor can he be compelled to give evidence against himself; that no man be deprived of his liberty, except by the law of the land or the judgment of his peers.

SEC. 9. That excessive bail ought not to be required, nor excessive fines imposed, nor cruel and unusual punishments inflicted.

SEC. 10. That general warrants, whereby an officer or messenger may be commanded to search suspected places without evidence of a fact committed, or to seize any person or persons not named, or whose offence is not particularly described and supported by evidence, are grievous and oppressive, and ought not to be granted.

SEC. 11. That in controversies respecting property, and in suits between man and man, the ancient trial by jury is preferable to any other, and ought to be held sacred.

SEC. 12. That the freedom of the press is one of the great bulwarks of liberty, and can never be restrained but by despotic governments.

SEC. 13. That a well-regulated militia, composed of the body of the people, trained to arms, is the proper, natural, and safe defence of a free State; that standing armies, in time of peace, should be avoided, as dangerous to liberty; and that in all cases the military should be under strict subordination to, and governed by, the civil power.

SEC. 14. That the people have a right to uniform government; and, therefore, that no government separate from, or independent of the government of Virginia, ought to be erected or established within the limits thereof.

SEC. 15. That no free government, or the blessings of

liberty, can be preserved to any people, but by a firm adherence to justice, moderation, temperance, frugality, and virtue, and by frequent recurrence to fundamental principles.

SEC. 16. That religion, or the duty which we owe to our Creator, and the manner of discharging it, can be directed only by reason and conviction, not by force or violence; and therefore all men are equally entitled to the free exercise of religion, according to the dictates of conscience; and that it is the mutual duty of all to practise Christian forbearance, love, and charity towards each other.

— Document No. 6 —

STATUTE OF VIRGINIA FOR RELIGIOUS FREEDOM, 1786[6]

After adoption of the Declaration of Independence by the Second Continental Congress, Jefferson retired from that body to accept election to the lower house of the Virginia assembly. There he advocated several reforms, including a bill to disestablish the Anglican Church. The measure became law in 1779, but Jefferson and some of his colleagues thought that divorcement of church and state did not go far enough. He proposed another measure to guarantee complete religious freedom. It did not become law until 1786, while Jefferson was minister to France. He regarded the statute for religious freedom, the Declaration of Independence, and the founding of

[6] W. W. Hening, ed., *Statutes at Large of Virginia*, XII, 84-86.

the University of Virginia as his three significant contributions.

✓ ✓ ✓

An act for establishing religious freedom.

I. WHEREAS Almighty God hath created the mind free; that all attempts to influence it by temporal punishments or burthens, or by civil incapacitations, tend only to beget habits of hypocrisy and meanness, and are a departure from the plan of the Holy author of our religion, who being Lord both of body and mind, yet chose not to . . . propagate it by coercions on either, as was in his Almighty power to do; that the impious presumption of legislators and rulers, civil as well as ecclesiastical, who being themselves but fallible and uninspired men, have assumed dominion over the faith of others, setting up their own opinions and modes of thinking as the only true and infallible, and as such endeavouring to impose them on others, hath established and maintained false religions over the greatest part of the world, and through all time; that to compel a man to furnish contributions of money for the propagation of opinions which he disbelieves, is sinful and tyrannical; that even the forcing him to support this or that teacher of his own religious persuasion, is depriving him of the comfortable liberty of giving his contributions to the particular pastor, whose morals he would make his pattern, and whose powers he feels most persuasive to righteousness, and is withdrawing from the ministry those temporary rewards, which proceeding from an approbation of their personal conduct, are an additional incitement to earnest and unremitting labours for the instruction of mankind; that our civil rights have no dependence on our religious opinions, any more than our opinions in physics or geometry; that therefore the proscribing any citizen as unworthy the public confidence by laying upon him an incapacity of being called to offices of trust and emolument, unless he profess or renounce this or that religious opinion, is depriving him injuriously of those privileges and advantages to which in common with his fellow-citizens he has a natural right; that it tends only to corrupt the principles of that religion it is meant to encourage, by bribing with a monopoly of wor[l]dly honours and emoluments, those who will externally profess and conform to it; that though indeed these are criminal who do not withstand such temptation, yet neither are those innocent who lay the bait in their way; that to suffer the civil magistrate to intrude his powers into the field of opinion, and to restrain the profession or propagation of principles on supposition of their ill tendency, is a dangerous fallacy, which at once destroys all religious liberty, because he being of course judge of that tendency will make his opinions the rule of judgment, and approve or condemn the sentiments of others only as they shall square with or differ from his own; that it is time enough for the rightful purposes of civil government, for its officers to interfere when principles break out into overt acts against peace and good order; and finally, that truth is great and will prevail if left to herself; that she is the proper and sufficient antagonist to error, and has nothing to fear from the conflict, unless by human interposition disarmed of her natural weapons, free argument and debate, errors ceasing to be dangerous when it is permitted freely to contradict them:

II. Be it enacted by the General Assembly, That no man shall be compelled to frequent or support any religious worship, place, or ministry whatsoever, nor shall be enforced, restrained, molested, or burthened in his body or goods, nor shall otherwise suffer on account of his religious opinions or belief; but that all men shall be free to profess, and by argument to maintain, their opinion in matters of religion, and that the same shall in no wise diminish, enlarge, or affect their civil capacities.

III. And though we well know that this assembly elected by the people for the ordinary purposes of legislation only, have no power to restrain the acts of succeeding assemblies, constituted with powers equal to our own, and that therefore to declare this act to be irrevocable would be of no effect in law; yet we are free to declare, and do declare, that the rights hereby asserted are of the natural rights of mankind, and that if any act shall be hereafter passed to repeal the present, or to narrow its operation, such act will be an infringement of natural right.

— Document No. 7 —

DIARY OF A MISSISSIPPI COTTON AND CORN PLANTER, 1856[7]

Eli J. Capell of "Pleasant Hill" plantation in southern Mississippi kept a diary for at least a quarter century (1842-1867), faithfully recording the chief concerns of daily routine. A typical page indicates what the owner of more than two thousand acres and seventy slaves thought worthy of entry. Hundreds of planters kept similar diaries and miscellaneous records.

✓   ✓   ✓

2nd Sunday [Nov. 2, 1856], A warm cloudy day with appearance of rain. I and family went to Bethany Church. Our family are all well and the Country remarkably healthy

3rd Monday. A very warm and Showery day with thunder & lightning at dark. I working all day setting up my Atwood Gin Stand 4 Boys packed out 5 Bales Cotton. 2 Boys hauled in Some fodder all the others picked *Peas* and finished all I have to pick I think I have saved 50 or 60 Bushels in all

4# Tuesday. A cold windy day I at Presidential Election all day The men cleared some land & one Team hauled in 6 Loads Corn & others picked Some Cotton in Dority field. This Corn Came from Gin field & the first hauled in from that field

5# Wednesday. A white Frost and cool windy day. I started my new Atwood Gin. All my hands picked Cotton in Dority field 1700 lbs

[7] Eli J. Capell Diary, Louisiana State University Department of Archives (Baton Rouge).

6# Thursday. A large white Frost with Some *Ice* the first this winter Gin going to day. The other hands picked Cotton in Dority field 1989 lbs Sim making negro Shoes & George working on Cabin Chimney frames

7# Friday. A very warm day & showery all day and tremendous rain in evening and after dark with lightning & thunder. 4 boys packed 2 Bales to make out a load & the Gin run. Ox Team Started after noon to Clinton with 7 Bales Cotton. The other hands picked Cotton in Dority field 400 lbs and in Orchard field 150 lbs The Boys cleared after Noon. Women finished picking Peas

8# Saturday. A Cold windy day. Gin going. The Boys cleared land & the Women & Some men hauled in 6 Loads of Corn. Sim making Shoes. George framing cabin Chimneys

— Document No. 8 —

AN ENGLISH GEOLOGIST'S VIEW OF HOPETON PLANTATION AND SOUTHERN SOCIETY, 1845-1846[8]

A London geologist, Sir Charles Lyell, observed everything from alligators to poison ivy as he toured the South in 1845-1846. Hopeton plantation, on the Altamaha River in Georgia, belonged to James Hamilton Couper, experimental agriculturist, with whom Lyell corresponded on geological subjects. The traveler, search-

[8] Charles Lyell, *A Second Visit to the United States of North America* (2 vols.; New York, 1849), I, 261-266.

ing for scientific knowledge, recorded a sympathetic account of Southern society.

✓   ✓   ✓

During a fortnight's stay at Hopeton, we had an opportunity of seeing how the planters live in the south, and the condition and prospects of the negroes on a well-managed estate. The relation of the slaves to their owners resembles nothing in the northern states. There is an hereditary regard and often attachment on both sides, more like that formerly existing between lords and their retainers in the old feudal times of Europe, than to any thing now to be found in America. The slaves identify themselves with the master, and their sense of their own importance rises with his success in life. But the responsibility of the owners is felt to be great, and to manage a plantation with profit is no easy task; so much judgment is required, and such a mixture of firmness, forbearance, and kindness. The evils of the system of slavery are said to be exhibited in their worst light when new settlers come from the free states. . . . To one who arrives in Georgia direct from Europe, with a vivid impression on his mind of the state of the peasantry there in many populous regions, their ignorance, intemperance, and improvidence, the difficulty of obtaining subsistence, and the small chance they have of bettering their lot, the condition of the black laborers on such a property as Hopeton, will afford but small ground for lamentation or despondency. I had many opportunities, while here, of talking with the slaves alone, or seeing them at work. I may be told that this was a favorable specimen of a well-managed estate; if so, I may at least affirm that mere chance led me to pay this visit, that is to say, scientific objects wholly unconnected with the "domestic institutions" of the south. . . . I can but relate what passed under my own eyes, or what I learnt from good authority, concealing nothing.

There are 500 negroes on the Hopeton estate, a great many of whom are children, and some old and superannuated. The latter class, who would be supported in a poor-house in England, enjoy here, to the end of their days, the society of their neighbors and kinsfolk, and live at large in separate houses assigned to them. The children have no regular work to do till they are ten or twelve years old. . . . When the mothers are at work, the young children are looked after by an old negress, called Mom Diana. . . . The parents indulge their own fancies in naming their children, and display a singular taste; for one is called January, another April, a third Monday, and a fourth Hard Times. The fisherman on the estate rejoices in the appellation of "Old Bacchus." Quash is the name of the favorite preacher, and Bulally the African name of another negro.

The out-door laborers have separate houses provided for them; even the domestic servants, except a few who are nurses to the white children, live apart from the great house—an arrangement not always convenient for the masters, as there is no one to answer a bell after a certain hour. . . . The laborers begin work at six o'clock in the morning, have an hour's rest at nine for breakfast, and many have finished their assigned task by two o'clock, all of them by three o'clock. In summer they divide their work differently, going to bed in the middle of the day, then rising to finish their task, and afterward spending a great part of the night in chatting, merry-making, preaching, and psalm-singing. At Christmas they claim a week's holidays, when they hold a kind of Saturnalia, and the owners can get no work done. Although there is scarcely any drinking, the master rejoices when this season is well over without mischief. The negro houses are as neat as the greater part of the cottages in Scotland (no flattering compliment it must be confessed), are provided always with a back door, and a hall, as they call it, in which is a chest, a table, two or three chairs, and a few shelves for crockery. . . . A little yard is often attached, in which are seen their chickens, and usually a yelping cur, kept for their amusement.

The winter, when the whites enjoy the best health, is the trying season for the negroes, who are rarely ill in the rice-grounds in summer, which are so fatal to the whites, that when the planters who have retreated to the sea-islands revisit their estates once a fortnight, they dare not sleep at home. Such is the indifference of the

negroes to heat, that they are often found sleeping with
their faces upward in a broiling sun, instead of lying
under the shade of a tree hard by. We visited the hospital at Hopeton, which consists of three separate wards,
all perfectly clean and well-ventilated. One is for men,
another for women, and a third for lying-in women. . . .

The negro mothers are often so ignorant or indo-
lent, that they cannot be trusted to keep awake and
administer medicine to their own children; so that the
mistress has often to sit up all night with a sick negro
child. In submitting to this, they are actuated by mixed
motives—a feeling of kindness, and a fear of losing the
services of the slave; but these attentions greatly attach
the negroes to their owners. In general, they refuse to
take medicine from any other hands but those of their
master or mistress. The laborers are allowed Indian meal,
rice, and milk, and occasionally pork and soup. As their
rations are more than they can eat, they either return
part of it to the overseer, who makes them an allowance
of money for it at the end of the week, or they keep it
to feed their fowls, which they usually sell, as well as
their eggs, for cash, to buy molasses, tobacco, and other
luxuries. When disposed to exert themselves, they get
through the day's task in five hours, and then amuse
themselves in fishing, and sell the fish they take; or some
of them employ their spare time in making canoes out
of large cypress trees, leave being readily granted them
to remove such timber, as it aids the landowner to clear
the swamps. They sell the canoes for about four dollars,
for their own profit. . . .

One day, when walking alone, I came upon a "gang"
of negroes, who were digging a trench. They were super-
intended by a black "driver," who held a whip in his
hand. . . . The names of gangs and drivers are odious,
and the sight of the whip was painful to me as a mark of
degradation, reminding me that the lower orders of
slaves are kept to their work by mere bodily fear, and
that their treatment must depend on the individual character of the owner or overseer. That the whip is rarely
used, and often held for weeks over them, merely *in ter-
rorem,* is, I have no doubt, true on all well governed
estates; and it is not that formidable weapon which I

have seen exhibited as formerly in use in the West Indies.
It is a thong of leather, half an inch wide and a quarter
of an inch thick. . . . The most severe punishment required in the last forty years, for a body of 500 negroes
at Hopeton, was for the theft of one negro from another. In that period there has been no criminal act of
the highest grade, for which a delinquent could be committed to the penitentiary in Georgia, and there have
been only six cases of assault and battery. As a race, the
negroes are mild and forgiving, and by no means so
prone to indulge in drinking as the white man or the
Indian. There were more serious quarrels, and more
broken heads, among the Irish in a few years, when they
came to dig the Brunswick Canal, than had been known
among the negroes in all the surrounding plantations
for half a century.

— Document No. 9 —

FREDERICK LAW OLMSTED
OBSERVES RICE PRODUCTION,
1853-1854[9]

*Frederick Law Olmsted, ambitious to become a mem-
ber of the "Republic of Letters," journeyed through the
South in 1853-1854, observing its agricultural economy
with the practiced eye of an experienced traveler. Three
publications followed his travels: on the seaboard slave
states, on Texas, and on the back country. A fourth
work,* The Cotton Kingdom, *combining previous books,*

[9] Frederick Law Olmsted, *A Journey in the Seaboard Slave
States, with Remarks on Their Economy* (New York,
1856), pp. 466-476.

appeared on the eve of the Civil War. His observations were friendly but critical. In the following informative account, he surveys rice production.

✓   ✓   ✓

In such a situation, the rice fields are first constructed as follows: Their outline being determined upon, the trees are cut upon it for a space of fifty feet in width; a ditch is then dug at the ebb of the water, the earth thrown out from which soon suffices to prevent the return of ordinary tides, and the laborers are thus permitted to work uninterruptedly. An embankment is then formed, upon the site of the first made ditch, sufficiently thick and high to resist the heaviest floods which can be anticipated. It is usually five feet in height, and fifteen in breadth at the base, and all stumps and roots are removed from the earth of which it is formed, as, in digging the first ditch, they have been from its base. The earth for it is obtained by digging a great ditch fifteen or twenty feet inside of it; and if more is afterwards needed, it is brought from a distance, rather than lessen its security by loosening the ground near its base.

While this embanking has been going on, the trees may have been felled over all the ground within, and, with the underbrush, drawn into piles or rows. At a dry time in the spring, fire is set to the windward side of these, and they are more or less successfully consumed. Often the logs remain, as do always the stumps, encumbering the rice field for many years. Usually, too, the larger trees are only girdled, and their charred or rotting trunks stand for years, rueful corpses of the old forests.

The cleared land is next divided into fields of convenient size, by embankments similar to, but not so large as, the main river embankment, the object of them being only to keep the water that is to be let into one field out of the next, which may not be prepared for it; commonly they are seven or eight feet wide at base and three feet high, with ditches of proportionate size adjoining them; a margin of eight or ten feet being left between the ditches and the embankments. Each field must be provided with a separate trunk and gate, to let in or exclude the water of the river; and if it is a back field, a canal,

embanked on either side, is sometimes . . . made for
this purpose. Such a canal is generally made wide enough
to admit of the passage of a scow for the transportation
of the crop.

These operations being concluded, the cultivation of
the land is commenced; but . . . it [is] necessary to
provide more ditches to remove the water, after a flooding of the field, with sufficient rapidity and complete-
ness. These ditches, which are, perhaps, but two feet
wide and deep, are dug between the crops, from time to
time, until all the fields are divided into rectangular beds
of a half or a quarter acre each. Now, when the gates
are open, at the fall of tide, any water that is on the
beds flows rapidly into these minor drains (or "quarter
ditches"), from these into the outside ditches of each
field, and from these through the field trunks into the
canal, or the main embankment ditch, and from this
through the main trunk into the river. The gates in the
trunk are made with valves, that are closed by the rise
of water in the river, so as not to again admit it. Another
set of gates, provided with valves opening the other
way, are shut down, and the former are drawn up,
when it is wished to admit the water, and to prevent its
outflow. . . .

There is another circumstance, however, connected
with the character of the season for rain, that still more
essentially concerns the interests of the rice planters,
especially those nearest the ocean. In a very dry season,
the rivers being low, the ocean water, impregnated
with salt, is carried further up than usual. Salt is poison-
ous to the rice plant; while, on the other hand, unless it
is flooded from the river, no crop can be made. The
longer the drought continues, the greater this difficulty
becomes, and the higher up it extends. . . .

In preparing the ground for the crop, it is first thoroughly "chopped," as the operation with the thick,
clumsy, heavy hoe is appropriately termed. This rudely
turns, mixes, and levels the surface, two or three inches
in depth. It is repeated as near as possible to the planting time, the soil being made as fine and friable, by crush-
ing the clods, as possible—whence this second hoeing is
termed the "mash." From the middle of March to the first

of April planting commences, the first operation in which is opening drills, or, as it is termed on the plantation, "trenching." This is done with narrow hoses, the drills or trenches being chopped out about four inches wide, two inches deep, and thirteen inches apart. To guide the trenchers, a few drills are first opened by expert hands, four feet four inches apart, stakes being set to direct them; the common hands then open two between each of these guide rows, measuring the distance only by the eye. The accuracy with which the lines are made straight is said to be astonishing; and this, as well as the ploughing, and many other operations performed by negroes, as I have had occasion to notice with colored laborers at the North, no less than among the slaves, indicates that the race generally has a good "mathematical eye," much more so at least than the Irish.

As fast as the trenches are made, light hands follow, strewing the seed in them. It is sowed very thickly through the breadth of the trenches, so that from two to three bushels of rice are used upon an acre. The seed is lightly covered with hoes as rapidly as possible after it is sowed. . . .

The force employed must always be large enough to complete the sowing of each field on the day it is begun. The outer gate in the trunk is opened as soon as the sowing is finished; and on the next rise of tide the water flows in, fills the ditches, and gradually rises until the whole ground is covered.

This is termed the "sprout flow," and the water is left on the field until the seed sprouts—from a week to a fortnight, according to the warmth of the season. It is then drawn off, and the field is left until the points of the shoots of the young plants appear above ground, when the second flooding is given it, called the "point flow." At this time, the water remains on till all the grass and weeds that have come up with the rice are killed, and until the rice itself is three or four inches in hight, and so strong that the birds cannot pull it up. As soon as the ground is sufficiently dry, after the "point flow," the rice is hoed, and a fortnight or three weeks later it is hoed again, remaining dry in the meantime. As soon, after the second hoeing, as the weeds are killed by the sun (or, if rainy weather, immediately, so as to float them off), the field is again flooded, the water being allowed to rise at first well above all the plants, that the weeds and rubbish which will float may drift to the sides of the field, where they are raked out, dried, and burned: the water is then lowered, so that the points of the rice may be seen above it. The rice will be from six inches to one foot in hight at this time, and the water remains on at the same hight for two or three weeks. The exact time for drawing it off is determined by the appearance of the rice, and is a point requiring an experienced and discreet judgment to decide. This is called the "long flow."

The field is again left to dry, after which it receives a third and a fourth hoeing, and, when it is judged to need it, the water is again let on to a depth that will not quite cover the rice, and now remains on till harvest.

The negroes are employed, until the rice is headed, in wading through it, and collecting and bringing out in baskets any aquatic grasses or volunteer rice that have grown in the trenches. "Volunteer rice" is such as is produced by seed that has remained on the ground during the winter, and is of such inferior quality that, if it is left to be threshed with the crop, it injures its salable value much more than the addition it makes to its quantity is worth.

When the rice has headed, the water is raised still higher, for the purpose of supporting the heavy crop, and to prevent the straw from being tangled or "laid" by the wind, until it is ripe for the sickle. . . .

The rice-harvest commences early in September. The water having been all drawn off the field [at] the previous ebb tide, the negroes reap the rice with sickles, taking three or four rows of it at a cut. The stubble is left about a foot in hight, and the rice is laid across the top of it, so that it will dry rapidly. One or two days afterwards it is tied in small sheaves, and then immediately carried to the barn or stack-yard. This is often some miles distant; yet the whole crop of many plantations is transported to it on the heads of the laborers. This work, at the hottest season of the year, in the midst of the recently exposed mire of the rice fields, is acknowledged to be exceedingly severe, and must be very hazardous to the health, even of negroes. . . .

The rice is neatly stacked, much as wheat is in Scotland, in round, thatched stacks. Threshing commences immediately after harvest, and on many plantations proceeds very tediously, in the old way of threshing wheat, with flails, by hand, occupying the best of the plantation force for the most of the winter. It is done on an earthen floor, in the open air, and the rice is cleaned by carrying it on the heads of the negroes, by a ladder, up on to a platform, twenty feet from the ground, and pouring it slowly down, so that the wind will drive off the chaff, and leave the grain in a heap, under the platform. But on most large plantations, threshing-machines, much the same as are used with us, driven either by horse-power or by steam-power, have been lately adopted, of course with great economy. Where horse-power is used for threshing, the wind is still often relied upon for removing the chaff, as of old; but where steam-engines are employed, there are often connected with the threshing-mill, very complete separators and fanners, together with elevators and other labor-saving machinery, some of it the best for such purposes that I have ever seen. . . .

After the ordinary threshing and cleaning from chaff, the rice still remains covered with a close, rough husk, which can only be removed by a peculiar machine, that lightly pounds it, so as to crack the husk without breaking the rice. Many of the largest plantations are provided with these mills, but it is now found more profitable (where the expense of procuring them has not been already incurred), to sell the rice "in the rough," as it is termed, before the husk is removed. There are very extensive rice-hulling mills in most large towns in Europe and America. . . .

The usual crop of rice is from thirty to sixty bushels from an acre, but even as high as one hundred bushels is sometimes obtained. Its weight (in the rough) is from forty-one to forty-nine pounds per bushel. The usual price paid for it (in the rough), in Charleston and Savannah, is from eighty cents to one dollar a bushel.

Planters usually employ their factors—merchants residing in Charleston, Savannah, or Wilmington, the three rice ports—to sell their crop by sample. The purchasers are merchants, or mill-owners, or the agents of foreign rice mills. These factors are also employed by the planters as their general business agents, making the necessary purchase of stores and stock for their plantation and family supply. Their commission is 2½ per cent.

Rice is used in the rice district as a constant article of food, never being absent from the breakfast and dinner table of many families. On the rice plantations, particularly those furnished with a hulling-mill, it is given a good deal to the negroes, more especially during the seasons of their harvest labor, and at the holidays. From this circumstance, I judge that it is thought better food than maize, although the cracked and inferior rice, that would be unmerchantable, is alone given them. . . . Rice is screened after the hull is removed, so as to produce several different classes, the difference in which is mainly in size, the lower denominations including only chips and powder of the grain. . . .

— Document No. 10 —

A KIDNAPPED NEGRO DESCRIBES SLAVE TRADING IN NEW ORLEANS, 1841 [10]

Solomon Northrup, a New York free Negro kidnapped into slavery, labored on Louisiana plantations for a dozen years before his release was effected. He

[10] *Twelve Years a Slave. Narrative of Solomon Northrup* (Auburn and Buffalo, 1854), pp. 78-82.

gives a realistic description of transactions in a New Orleans slave pen.

✓   ✓   ✓

In the first place we were required to wash thoroughly, and those with beards, to shave. We were then furnished with a new suit each, cheap, but clean. The men had hat, coat, shirt, pants and shoes; the women frocks of calico, and handkerchiefs to bind about their heads. We were now conducted into a large room in the front part of the building to which the yard was attached, in order to be properly trained, before the admission of customers. The men were arranged on one side of the room, the women on the other. The tallest was placed at the head of the row, then the next tallest, and so on in the order of their respective heights. Emily was at the foot of the line of women. [Theophilus] Freeman charged us to remember our places, exhorted us to appear smart and lively,— sometimes threatening, and again, holding out various inducements. During the day he exercised us in the art of "looking smart," and of moving to our places with exact precision.

After being fed, in the afternoon, we were again paraded and made to dance. Bob, a colored boy, who had some time belonged to Freeman, played on the violin. Standing near him, I made bold to inquire if he could play the "Virginia Reel." He answered he could not, and asked me if I could play. Replying in the affirmative, he handed me the violin. I struck up a tune, and finished it. Freeman ordered me to continue playing, and seemed well pleased, telling Bob that I far excelled him—a remark that seemed to grieve my musical companion very much.

Next day many customers called to examine Freeman's "new lot." The latter gentleman was very loquacious, dwelling at much length upon our several good points and qualities. He would make us hold up our heads, walk briskly back and forth, while customers would feel of our hands and arms and bodies, turn us about, ask us what we could do, make us open our mouths and show our teeth, precisely as a jockey examines a horse which he is to barter for or purchase.

Sometimes a man or woman was taken back to the small house in the yard, stripped, and inspected more minutely. Scars upon a slave's back were considered evidence of a rebellious or unruly spirit, and hurt his sale.

An old gentleman, who said he wanted a coachman, appeared to take a fancy to me. From his conversation with Freeman, I learned he was a resident in the city. I very much desired that he would buy me, because I conceived it would not be difficult to make my escape from New-Orleans on some northern vessel. Freeman asked him fifteen hundred dollars for me. The old gentleman insisted it was too much as times were very hard. Freeman, however, declared that I was sound and healthy, of a good constitution, and intelligent. He made it a point to enlarge upon my musical attainments. The old gentleman argued quite adroitly that there was nothing extraordinary about the nigger, and finally, to my regret, went out, saying he would call again. During the day, however, a number of sales were made. David and Caroline were purchased together by a Natchez planter. They left us, grinning broadly, and in the most happy state of mind, caused by the fact of their not being separated. Lethe was sold to a planter of Baton Rouge, her eyes flashing with anger as she was led away.

The same man also purchased Randall. The little fellow was made to jump, and run across the floor, and perform many other feats, exhibiting his activity and condition. All the time the trade was going on, Eliza was crying aloud, and wringing her hands. She besought the man not to buy him, unless he also bought herself and Emily. She promised, in that case, to be the most faithful slave that ever lived. The man answered that he could not afford it, and then Eliza burst into a paroxysm of grief, weeping plaintively. Freeman turned round to her, savagely, with his whip in his uplifted hand, ordering her to stop her noise, or he would flog her. He would not have such work—such snivelling; and unless she ceased that minute, he would take her to the yard and give her a hundred lashes. Yes, he would take the nonsense out of her pretty quick—if he didn't, might he be d——d. Eliza shrunk before him, and tried to wipe away her tears, but it was all in vain. She wanted to be with her

children, she said, the little time she had to live. All the
frowns and threats of Freeman, could not wholly silence
the afflicted mother. She kept on begging and beseech-
ing them, most piteously, not to separate the three. Over
and over again she told them how she loved her boy. A
great many times she repeated her former promises—
how very faithful and obedient she would be; how hard
she would labor day and night, to the last moment of her
life, if he would only buy them altogether. But it was of
no avail; the man could not afford it. The bargain was
agreed upon, and Randall must go alone. Then Eliza ran
to him; embraced him passionately; kissed him again and
again; told him to remember her—all the while her tears
falling in the boy's face like rain.

— Document No. 11 —

NEW ORLEANS AND ITS LEVEE IN 1844[11]

*For reasons of health, young Henry B. Whipple,
future Protestant Episcopal Bishop of Minnesota, left
his New York home in 1843 for a tour of the South and
West. His analytical mind and descriptive talent are illustrated by his impressions of New Orleans, its commercial activity, and its diverse humanity.*

✓   ✓   ✓

Tuesday 27, February 1844   Today I visited the levee,
and saw this mart of business. Such a motley crowd one

[11] *Bishop Whipple's Southern Diary, 1843-1844,* edited by
Lester B. Shippee (University of Minnesota Press).
Copyright 1937 held by the University of Minnesota.
Pp. 95-97, 118-119.

seldom sees. The levee is about one mile long at its widest place & 200 yards wide. Here steamers, flat boats and vessels discharge their freight, and you see an innumerable quantity of barrels, hogsheads, cotton bags, pork hams, apples, bagging & rope &c &c. In fact this same levee is the market place of the wealth of the west. Nowhere in the U.S. is there such an amount of business going on as here. And then the speckled & streaked appearance of those engaged about it adds much to the scene. Drays innumerable in number are engaged in transporting merchandise to & from the levee and one is astonished at the immense numbers of these carts used. There are in the city over 4000 of them and these find steady and constant employ. This levee has been mostly made by soil washed up by the Mississippi which here has a powerful & rapid current the force of which is nearly 4 miles per hour. It is a beautiful sight to stand on the upper deck of a steamer and look around you and watch the movements of the busy bustling throng at your feet. Every variety of character can here be seen from the curious Yankee like myself to the busy restless speculator who makes this levee his world of action. Negroes of all shades from the Guinea black to the pale sickly looking quadroon, aristocratic niggers with gold chains & satin vests and working niggers, fat laughing niggers and thin sallow faced negroes who look as solemn as if they never smiled. Old men and young men, hoosiers, pukes, buckeyes, crackers, greenies, busters and other varieties of civilization are here exhibited in all the eccentricities of their individual character. Every variety of business appears to be carried on . . . and about the levee. Steamers, schooners, flat boats & ships here lie side by side & here the salt and fresh water tar meet. In one part of the levee you may hear the cracked voice of some bustling autioneer and close by see a quiet sedate business man who ever keeps on the calm & quiet side of business & gets his fortune by patience & industry. Such varieties of that peculiar species yclept loafers can nowhere else be found in the south. What scant specimens of humanity; as you gaze on them you wonder if it can be that these are immortal beings and the noble beasts of burden around them perishable. Such half putrïd masses

of matter in their ragged tattered dress, their rimless
hats, their airy boots, their long matted hair & unshaven
beard. Can it be these things ever had a home, ever had
mothers, brothers and sisters as others. To see them
lounging on cotton bales, whiskey barrels, enjoying the
scorching rays of the sun, you would fancy not. They
have no ideas that do not savor of whiskey & laziness. No
employment, no friends, no home. Life is to them a
dreamy blank & death is to them the end of being. They
have no fear of undertakers, no dread of coffins, for to
them these appurtenances of death are obsolete. The
dissecting room or the Mississippi is their grave. Every
nation appears to be represented in this mart of business, from the hardy Scotch & Swede of the north to the
tawney Maltese of a warmer clime, each jabbering away
in his native tongue like so many monkeys. All grades of
society, all classes here mingle & commingle in all the
peculiarity of their individual character; as a western
buster would say "stranger, if you want a tall walk &
want to seet all sight go for an hour on the levee." And
he who has not seen the New Orleans levee has not seen
all of this great country. . . .

The truth is New Orleans appears to me to be at the
extreme of everything, the hottest, the dirtiest, the most
sickly, and at times the most healthy, the busiest, and the
most dull, the most wicked & the most orderly. They have
in truth the most business, the best of land, the prettiest
of women, the fastest of horses and the most delightful
climate. It rains harder, it is more dusty. It is hotter and
has a more diversified people than any city in the union.
Changes take place here with almost the rapidity of
thought. Today rich, tomorrow poor, today well, tomorrow dead, today hot, tomorrow cold, today dry, tomorrow wet, suffocating for air one day and the next suf-
fering from extreme winds which almost vie with a hurri-
cane in their fierceness. You can see here some of the
richest & some of the poorest of humanity. They have
here the first class of business talent as well as the "ne
plus ultra" of loaferism. Dandies of the first water and
backwoodsmen who care not for dress. Men of the highest intellect & fools of the first class. An observing man
can see as much of the world & of diversified character

here as in any city in the union. It is the grand reservoir
of the great West. Millions of property yearly find their
way here. And one steamer has hardly arrived before
you hear in the distance the hoarse cough of another
of these floating houses loaded with produce & teeming
with busy restless mortals, and from one horn of the
crescent to the other ships & other water craft lie in
close contiguity. . . .

— Document No. 12 —

A DAY IN THE RURAL SOUTH WITH HARRIET MARTINEAU, 1834[12]

*Prolific writer on sundry subjects, Harriet Marti-
neau toured the South in the winter of 1834-1835. She
was graciously entertained despite the fact that she
had already expressed strong antislavery views. Publication of* Society in America *followed her return to England; a second work,* Retrospect of Western Travel, *was
more successful. Her description of rural life is quite
likely a composite picture.*

↗   ↗   ↗

Our stationary rural life in the South was various and
pleasant enough; all shaded with the presence of slavery, but without any other drawback. There is something in the make-shift, irregular mode of life where
there are slaves, that is amusing when the cause is forgotten.

[12] Harriet Martineau, *Retrospect of Western Travel* (2 vols.;
London, 1838), I, 214-223.

The waking in the morning is accomplished by two or three black women staring at you from the bedposts. Then it is five minutes' work to get them out of the room. Perhaps, before you are half dressed, you are summoned to breakfast. . . . After breakfast a farmer in homespun—blue trousers and an orange-brown coat, or all over gray—comes to speak with your host. A drunken white has shot one of his negroes, and he fears no punishment can be obtained, because there were no witnesses of the deed but blacks. A consultation is held whether the affair shall go into court; and, before the farmer departs, he is offered cake and liqueur.

Your hostess, meantime, has given her orders, and is now engaged in a back room, or out in the piazza behind the house, cutting out clothes for her slaves; very laborious work in warm weather. There may be a pretence of lessons among the young people, and something more than pretence if they happen to have a tutor or governess; but the probability is that their occupations are as various a their tempers. . . . Your hostess comes in at length, and you sit down at work with her; she gratifies your curiosity about her "people," telling you how soon they burn out their shoe's at the toes, and wear out their winter woollens, and tear up their summer cottons; and how impossible it is to get black women to learn to cut out clothes without waste; and how she never inquires when and where the whipping is done, as it is the overseer's business, and not hers. She has not been seated many minutes when he is called away, and returns saying how babyish these people are, that they will not take medicine unless she gives it to them; and how careless of each other, so that she has been obliged to stand by and see Diana put clean linen upon her infant, and to compel Bet to get her sick husband some breakfast.

Morning visitors next arrive. It may be the clergyman, with some new book that you want to look at; and inquires whether your host sees any prospect of getting the requisite number of professors for the new college, or whether the present head of the institution is to continue to fill all the chairs. It may be a lank judge from some raw district, with a quid in his cheek, a swordcane in his hand, and a legal doubt in his mind which he wants your host to resolve. It may be a sensible woman, with courtesy in her countenance and decision in her air, who is accustomed really to rule her household, and to make the most of such human material and such a human lot as are pressing around and upon her. . . .

. . . The carriage and saddle-horses are scrambling on the gravel before the door, and the children run in to know if they may ride with you. Cake, fruit, and liqueurs, or perhaps tea, are brought in, and then the ladies depart. The clergyman thinks he will ride round with your party, hearing that you are going to inspect Mr. A.'s plantation. He warns you that it will not be "pleasant to see even the best plantations," and your trembling heart fully agrees.

You admire the horsemanship of your host on his white horse, and the boys on their black ponies. The carriage goes at good speed, and yet the fast *pace* of the saddle-horses enables the party to keep together. While you are looking out upon a picturesque loghouse, peeping forth from a blossomy thicket, or admiring a splendid hedge of the Cherokee rose in straggling bloom, Rosa rouses herself from a revery, and asks you to tell her all about Victoria. . . .

Your host paces up to the carriage window to tell you that you are now on A.'s plantation. You are overtaking a long train of negroes going to their work from dinner. They look all over the colour of the soil they are walking on: dusky in clothing, dusky in complexion. An old man, blacker than the rest, is indicated to you as a native African; and you point out a child so light as to make you doubt whether he be a slave. . . .

You are now taken to the cotton-gin, the building to your left, where you are shown how the cotton, as picked from the pods, is drawn between cylinders so as to leave the seeds behind; and how it is afterward packed, by hard pressure, into bales. The neighbouring creek is damned up to supply the water-wheel by which this gin is worked. You afterward see the cotton-seed laid in handfuls round the stalks of the young springing corn, and used in the cotton field as manure.

Meantime you attempt to talk with the slaves. You ask how old that very aged man is, or that boy; they will give you no intelligible answer. Slaves never know, or never will tell their ages, and this is the reason why the census presents such extraordinary reports on this point, declaring a great number to be above a hundred years old. If they have a kind master, they will boast to you of how much he gave for each of them, and what sums he has refused for them. If they have a hard master, they will tell you that they would have more to eat and be less flogged, but that massa is busy, and has no time to come down and see that they have enough to eat. Your hostess is well known on this plantation, and her kind face has been recognised from a distance; and already a negro woman has come to her with seven or eight eggs, for which she knows she shall receive a quarter dollar. You follow her to the negro quarter, where you see a tidy woman knitting, while the little children who are left in her charge are basking in the sun, or playing all kinds of antics in the road; little shining, plump, clear-eyed children, whose mirth makes you sad when you look round upon their parents, and see what these bright creatures are to come to. You enter one of the dwellings, where everything seems to be of the same dusky hue: the crib against the wall, the walls themselves, and the floor, all look one yellow. More children are crouched round the wood fire, lying almost in the embers. . . .

You are then invited to see the house, learning by the way the extent and value of the estate you are visiting, and of the "force" upon it. You admire the lofty, cool rooms, with their green blinds, and the width of the piazzas on both sides the house, built to compensate for the want of shade from trees, which cannot be allowed near the dwelling for fear of moschetoes. You visit the icehouse, and find it pretty full, the last winter having been a severe one. You learn that, for three or four seasons after this icehouse was built, there was not a spike of ice in the state, and a cargo had to be imported from Massachusetts.

When you have walked in the field as long as the heat will allow, you step into the overseer's bare dwelling, within its bare enclosure, where fowls are strutting about, and refresh yourself with a small tumbler of milk; a great luxury, which has been ordered for the party. The overseer's fishing-tackle and rifle are on the wall, and there is a medicine chest and a shelf of books. He is tall, sallow, and *nonchalant*, dropping nothing more about himself and his situation than that he does not know that he has had more than his share of sickness and trouble in his vocation, and so he is pretty well satisfied. . . .

You are glad to find, on arriving at home, that you have half an hour to lie down before you dress, and are surprised, on rising, to feel how you are refreshed. You have not very far to go to dinner; only to Mr. E.'s cottage on the Sand Hills. . . .

The dinner is plentiful, including, of course, turkey, ham, and sweet potatoes; excellent claret, and large blocks of icecream. A slave makes gentle war against the flies with the enormous bunch of peacocks' feathers; and the agitation of the air is pleasant while the ladies are engaged in eating, so that they cannot use their own fans, which are hung by loops on the backs of their chairs. The afternoon is spent in the piazza, where coffee is served. There the ladies sit, whisking their feather fans, jesting with the children, and talking over the last English poem or American novel, or complaining bitterly of the dreadful incendiary publications which Mr. E. heard from Mr. H., who had heard it from Mr. M., that Judge R. had said that somebody had seen circulated among the negroes by some vile agent of the horrid abolitionists of the North.

You go in to tea, and find the table strewed with prints, and the piano open, and Mrs. F. plays and sings. The gentlemen have done discussing the French war and the currency, and are praising the conduct of the Committee of Vigilance; frankly informing you, as a stranger, of the reasons of its formation, and the modes of its operation in deterring abolitionists from coming into the neighbourhood, in arresting them on any suspicion of tampering with the negroes, and in punishing them summarily if any facts are established against them. . . .

Your host amuses you with anecdotes of South country life. He asks you how you were struck with Mrs. L., whose call you returned yesterday. You reply that she seems a cheerful, hearty personage, who makes the best of a poor lot; and you relate how pleased you were at the frankness with which she owned, pointing to the stocking she was darning, that she knew little of books nowadays, or of music, as she was making shirts and darning stockings for her sons all the year round. You were sorry to see such evidences of poverty; chairs with broken backs, and a piano with three legs, and a cracked flute; but glad that Mrs. L. seemed able to look on the bright side of things. Your host throws himself back, and laughs for three minutes; and, when he recovers, informs you that Mrs. L. is the wealthiest widow in the state. . . .

The storm abates. You are the oracle as to what o'clock it is; and, as you are confident that it is near eleven, the chamber lights are brought. You dismiss your dusky attendants, and throw yourself on your ample sofa for half an hour, to recall what you have seen and heard this day, and meditate on the scope and tendencies of Country Life in the Southern States.

— Document No. 13 —

A BRITISH ARISTOCRAT CENSURES SOUTH CAROLINA SOCIETY, 1828 [13]

Mrs. Basil (Margaret Hunter) Hall accompanied her husband to the United States in 1827-1828 and

[13] *The Aristocratic Journey: Being the Outspoken Letters of Mrs. Basil Hall Written during a Fourteen Months' Sojourn in America, 1827-1828,* ed. by Una Pope-Hennessy. Published by G. P. Putnam's Sons (New York, 1931), pp. 203-205, 207-209, 210, 212-213. Reprinted by permission.

recorded her impressions of American life in letters to her sister Jane. Previous travels in Italy and Spain led to odious comparisons of Northern as well as Southern society. Variations from standard etiquette at dinners and dances provided ample opportunity to disparage unrefined democratic customs despite hospitable reception wherever she traveled.

↗   ↗   ↗

[*February* 13, 1828] We have got pretty far South since I finished my last letter to you at Norfolk. We have in the interval had three days' hard travelling, by which I think Eliza is much the least fatigued of the party, and she is to-day running about looking as lively and as little heated as if she had not gone a mile, instead of having been bumped and banged and thumped about in a stage in a way that you may form some idea of if you remember the state of the roads across the Pyrenees. . . . After travelling twenty-eight miles we stopped to dine at Suffolk, and there paid for a much inferior dinner to what we should have had in the Northern or Eastern States, nearly twice as much as we should have been charged there. . . . The road during the whole day lay through a miserable country, pine barrens and swamps, with here and there a field of tobacco and cotton which showed us that we had got into a warmer latitude. But the most characteristic and the most disagreeable features were the immense numbers of blacks everywhere along the road, for being Sunday they were idle and straying about the roads. A more miserable looking race I never beheld, with hardly a rag to cover them, and they are so stupid and so slow that really one's patience is severely put to the test by them. The white population over that part of the country through which we have passed is almost as wretched in appearance as the black and, in my opinion, far more degraded, not one of them, as far as we have been able to learn, ever works. Most of them own two or three negroes whom they send out to work and pay them so much a day which they spend in brandy, for drinking is carried to a greater excess in the South even than it is in the North. The houses they live in are the most wretched hovels I ever saw in my life, log hovels not even weathertight; I am sure no Irish cabin can be poorer, and the people themselves look squalid and miserable. Their manners we found gruff and uncivil. . . .

February 22:—It was our intention to have set out today for Charleston, and we were actually all packed and ready, but it occurred to us early this morning that we were running away from the capital of the State [Columbia] with rather too little ceremony, and that we ought to bestow another day upon it. This has been the most perfectly beautiful day that I have seen for months, serene and clear with a bright warm sun. We went by appointment at ten o'clock to call at Dr. [Thomas] Cooper's, the President of the College; he is an Englishman by birth and was one of those who left his country at the time when the French Revolution caused so many disturbances in England. . . . The people here are very hospitable, which is indeed the character of all the Southern States. The Coopers wished us to make their house our home and Chancellor [Henry W.] de Saussure sent his carriage to me this morning to make what use I pleased of it the whole day. . . . We were asked to dine at the Governor's, Mr. [John] Taylor's, to a military ball by some officers, and to a party at Judge de Saussure's. . . . To the dinner we went at half past four, and I must say that in spite of all my experience of the strange arrangements of American dinners I confess this style did astonish me, and what any of you who have never seen such would have thought I cannot say. There was a huge party invited to meet us, all gentlemen with the exception of four ladies belonging to the house. . . . There was the same fuss before dinner of calling the mistress of the house out of the room and so on, and finally she and another elderly, female relation disappeared altogether and we found them standing ready placed at the upper end of the table, and then with one consent the gentlemen fell to carving the dishes nearest to them with a degree of dispatch and eagerness that I never saw equalled anywhere out of a steamboat. The top dish was a ham which Mrs. Taylor herself showed her power of carving upon by beginning to cut it in pieces from the knuckle upwards. The rest of the entertainment consisted of turkeys, roast and boiled, chickens, roast ducks, corned beef, and fish, together with various dishes of sweet potatoes, Irish potatoes, cabbage, rice, and beetroot, to demolish which we were furnished with two pronged forks, and if you were troublesome enough to call for a second knife you were furnished with one merely half wiped. For second course we had *eight pies* down the side of the table, six dishes of glasses of syllabub and as many of jelly, besides one or two "floating islands", as they denominate what we call whipped cream, and odd corners filled up by ginger and other preserves. I was fortunately well placed next an exceedingly agreeable old man, Judge De Saussure, a most gentlemanlike person. . . . We had neither tea nor coffee after dinner and at seven o'clock went off to the ball, but if the dinner was queer, what was the ball! . . . It is quite out of my power to describe it to you. The day was Washington's birthday, and I suppose that the ball was in honour of the occasion. The Military, that is to say the Militia, Yeomanry, and Volunteers, were all in uniform, which made the *gaucherie* of the individuals all the more conspicuous. Then the ladies I can compare to nothing I ever saw except girls at the circus or strolling players at the Dundee Theatre, dressed in my cast-off finery fitted up according to their own taste. Such heads, such fabrications of silver muslin and tinsel, such feathers and such flowers it would require the pen of a poet or the pencil of a painter to do justice to. I was asked by the Captain of the Troop to dance, but the honour I declined, fortunately, for I should have been strangely thrown out by what they imagine to be quadrilles but which a Frenchman, I think, would have scarce recognised. An hour of this was, you will believe, enough, and we were glad to exchange the ball for a party at Judge De Saussure's, where I had as tough an argument regarding slavery with some ladies as ever Basil had on any subject with gentlemen, and by ten o'clock we were at home. . . .

Charleston, South Carolina, February 26:—I went to see one sight to-day which I had not before had an opportunity of witnessing—an auction of slaves. There was an immense collection of them gathered together near the Post Office, from the balcony of which I saw it. A table was placed in the centre on which stood the auctioneers and the different lots as they were set up and knocked down to the highest bidder like so many books, chairs, or bullocks. There were multitudes of infants, little unconscious things, sleeping in their mothers' arms or smiling and laughing merrily, quite unaware of their own degradation. They were sold in families, which so far it was pleasant to see, but still it was a horrible sight. Close by were auctions of horses and carriages going on, so near indeed that it was impossible to distinguish whether the last bid was for the four-footed or the human animal. There was an expression of dogged indifference about the poor blacks, but I am told they do not at all like to be removed from the place where they have been brought up. . . .

On the twenty-ninth there was a ball given by the Jockey Club, to which we were invited and went. The room is good and was well lighted, nevertheless, it was a very dull ball, much too thinly attended and too small a proportion of gentlemen. . . . There were awful pauses between the dances, and the music was really insufferably bad. I had thought the young men much more gentlemanlike when I saw them in the morning than those generally to be seen in this country, but in the evening they looked very second-rate, indeed, more vulgar, I think, than most I have seen elsewhere. As for the female part of the company, I never in my life saw so many ugly women gathered together, there were but three pretty women in the room, two of them from Philadelphia, the other a French girl. . . .

Yesterday we had another stroll about the town which I admire the more I see of it, and when the trees which ornament the side of the streets are quite out the effect must be very pretty. It is a remarkably cheerful looking place, Charleston. The dinner at Mr. Pettigrew's consisted of thirteen gentlemen and three ladies, Mrs. Pettigrew, Mrs. Nott, who is living in the house, and myself, the others were all gentlemen without their wives, according to the fashion of the place and of many other places in the Union. Women are just looked upon as house-keepers in this country, and as such are allowed

to preside at the head of their own table, that they may
see that all goes right. . . . I must in justice say one
thing in favour of the South Carolinians, they are remarkably hospitable, not only in inviting strangers into
their houses, but lending their carriages, which is a much
less common piece of hospitality. . . .

— Document No. 14 —

MINT JULEPS, TOBACCO QUIDS, AND STRAWBERRIES, 1847[14]

*"Characters" were numerous on stagecoaches and
river boats in the South, and travelers with a sense of
humor often described them in exaggerated language.
The Scotsman Alexander Mackay, on his tour of the
United States in 1846-1847, met a loquacious Irishman on a steamboat trip from Montgomery to Mobile.
The quoted conversation may not be an exact reproduction, but the spirit of the piece seems realistic enough.*

✓   ✓   ✓

Amongst my fellow-passengers was a young Irishman,
whose ready wit, active fancy, and lively rattling conversation, went far to beguile the tedium of a long and
rather monotonous sail. He had been "caught young,"
as he said himself, having emigrated with his parents at a
very tender age to America. He was, when I met him,
the travelling agent of a large mercantile establishment
in New York, his occupation keeping him in almost
constant locomotion, and frequently leading him to the

[14] Alexander Mackay, *The Western World; or, Travels in the
    United States in 1846-47* (3 vols.; London, 1849), II,
    267-269.

South, with every portion of which he appeared to be well acquainted.

"You'll be going to New Orleens?" said he to me, as we were conversing together the first night in the saloon over a sherry-cobbler, previously to retiring for the night.

"That, for the present, is my destination," I replied.

"And a mighty fine place you'll find New Orleens to be," continued he; "indeed, I prefer it to all the other towns in the Union."

"That's strange," said I, "for in more than one respect its character is none of the best."

"Is it character you're speakin' off?" he rejoined; "sure there's no other town in the whole country where you'll find green peas in the month of January."

I could not but confess that in this at least there was nothing unfavourable to the town.

"And as for mint-juleps," he continued, "they begin to drink them there before winter has thought of going off for the season in the north. What think you of that?"

"That the sooner they begin they're the sooner over," said I; "besides, they have the satisfaction of beginning them in the north when you're tired of them at New Orleans."

"Yes, but you see you can enjoy that satisfaction with them, by going north with the juleps," he observed. "Nothing can be nicer than keeping on the track of the warm weather, and for weeks finding yourself only in the beginning of summer, drinking bumpers to it morning, noon, and night. Many's the time I have juleped it from New Orleans to Portland."

I could not but confess to the excellence of mint-juleps in hot weather, although I could not see the pleasure of being drenched with them. On observing this to him, he assured me that he was no slave to them, as he alternated pretty frequently between the julep, the cobbler, the phlegm-cutter, and the gin-sling.

"Besides," said he, "I like, when I can manage it, to take the strawberries along with them."

"What," said I, "then you have also travelled north with the strawberries?"

"That I have," he replied, "and nice companions they are, to be sure. They seemed to grow under my feet as I

went along, and I have sometimes almost lived on them
for days together. Yes," he continued, depositing his
quid into the spittoon at his feet, "I have dined on strawberries, and taken my baccy for a dessert."

"Which could you most easily dispense with," I asked,
"the strawberries or the tobacco?"

"That's as much as to say," said he, "which could you
most easily give up, a luxury or a necessity?"

"Do you place either in the category of necessaries?"
inquired I.

"I look on one of them as both a luxury and a necessity," he replied; "strawberries are a luxury, but tobacco
is as necessary to me as it is agreeable; I have chewed
since I was knee high to a goose, and will go on chewing until I'm a gone goose."

"I wish all your countrymen," I observed, "had as
ample means of appeasing their appetites as you have."

— Document No. 15 —

VICKSBURG AND ITS
HINTERLAND, 1835 [15]

*Joseph Holt Ingraham, a Maine "Yankee," lived
most of his adult life in the Southwest, serving as school-
teacher and clergyman in Mississippi and Tennessee. A
prolific novelist, he turned his attention occasionally to
other literary forms, among them* The South-West
(*1835*), *in which he described small farmer teamsters
who hauled their cotton bales to Vicksburg by ox-team.*

✓   ✓   ✓

There is no town in the south-west more flourishing
than Vicksburg. It is surrounded by rich plantations, and

[15] [Joseph Holt Ingraham], *The South-West. By a Yankee*
(2 vols. New York, 1835), II, 170-172.

contains many public-spirited individuals; whose co-operation in public enterprises is opening new avenues of wealth for the citizens, and laying a broad and secure foundation for the future importance of the town. It is already a powerful rival of Natchez: but the two places are so distant from each other, that their interests will always revolve in different circles. The situation of this town, on the shelving declivity of a cluster of precipitous hills, which rise abruptly from the river, is highly romantic. The houses are scattered in picturesque groups on natural terraces along the river, the balcony or portico of one often overhanging the roof of another. Merchandise destined for Clinton is landed here, and hauled over a hilly country to that place, a distance of thirty-five miles. Cotton is often conveyed to Vicksburg, and other shipping places, from a distance of one hundred miles in the interior. The cotton teams, containing usually ten bales, are drawn by six or eight yoke of oxen, which accomplish about twenty miles a day in good weather. The teamsters camp every night, in an enclosure formed by their waggons and cattle, with a bright fire burning; and occasionally their bivouacs present striking groups for the pencil. The majority of these teamsters are slaves; but there are many small farmers who drive their own oxen, often conveying their whole crop on one waggon. These small farmers form a peculiar class, and include the majority of the inhabitants in the east part of the state. With the awkwardness of the Yankee countryman, they are destitute of his morals, education, and reverence for religion. With the rude and bold qualities of the chivalrous Kentuckian, they are destitute of his intelligence, and the humour which tempers and renders amusing his very vices. They are in general uneducated, and their apparel consists of a coarse linsey-woolsey, of a dingy yellow or blue, with broadbrimmed hats; though they usually follow their teams bare-footed and bare-headed, with their long locks hanging over their eyes and shoulders, giving them a wild appearance. Accost them as they pass you, one after another, in long lines, cracking their whips, which they use instead of the goad—perhaps the turn-out of a whole district, from the old, gray-headed hunter, to the youngest boy that can wield the whip, often fifteen and twenty feet in length, including the staff—and their replies will generally be sullen or insulting. There is in them a total absence of that courtesy which the country people of New England manifest for strangers. They will seldom allow carriages to pass them, unless attended by gentlemen, who often have to do battle for the highway. Ladies, in carriages or on horse-back, if unattended by gentlemen, are most usually insulted by them. They have a decided aversion to a broad-cloth coat, and this antipathy is transferred to the wearer. There is a species of warfare kept up between them and the citizens of the shipping ports, mutually evinced by the jokes and tricks played upon them by the latter when they come into market; and their retaliation, when their hour of advantage comes, by an encounter in the back woods, which they claim as their domain. At home they live in log-houses on partially cleared lands, labor hard in their fields, sometimes owning a few slaves, but more generally with but one or none.—They are good hunters, and expert with the rifle, which is an important article of furniture in their houses. Whiskey is their favorite beverage, which they present to the stranger with one hand, while they give him a chair with the other. They are uneducated, and destitute of the regular administration of the gospel. As there is no common school system of education adopted in this state, their children grow up as rude and ignorant as themselves; some of whom, looking as wild as young Orsons, I have caught in the cotton market at Natchez, and questioned upon the simple principles of religion and education which every child is supposed to know, and have found them wholly uninformed.

— Document No. 16 —

WHITE SULPHUR SPRINGS, 1837[16]

The reputation of White Sulphur Springs in (West) Virginia equaled Saratoga's as a fashionable watering place in the ante-bellum era. Captain Frederick Marryat, English naval officer and novelist, described the resort in his American diary, based upon a visit to the United States and Canada in 1837-1838.

✓   ✓   ✓

We arrived first at the blue sulphur springs, and I remained there for one day to get rid of the dust of travelling. They have a very excellent hotel there, with a ball-room, which is open till eleven o'clock every night; the scenery is very pretty, and the company was good—as indeed is the company at all these springs, for they are too distant, and the travelling too expensive for every body to get there. But the blue sulphur are not fashionable, and the consequence was, we were not crowded, and were very comfortable. People who cannot get accommodated at the white sulphur, remain here until they can, the distance between them being only twenty-two miles.

The only springs which are fashionable are the white sulphur, and as these springs are a feature in American society, I shall describe them more particularly.

They are situated in a small valley, many hundred feet above the level of the sea, and are about fifteen or twenty acres in area, surrounded by small hills covered with foliage to their summits: at one end of the valley is the hotel, with the large dining-room for all the visitors.

[16] Frederick Marryat, *A Diary in America, with Remarks on Its Institutions* (2 vols.; Philadelphia, 1839), II, 6-9.

Close to the hotel, but in another building, is the ball-room, and a little below the hotel on the other side, is the spring itself; but beautiful as is the whole scenery, the great charm of this watering place is, the way in which those live who visit it. The rises of the hills which surround the valley are covered with little cottages, log-houses, and other picturesque buildings, sometimes in rows, and ornamented with verandahs, without a second story above, or kitchen below. Some are very elegant and more commodious than the rest, having been built by gentlemen who have the right given to them by the company to whom the springs belong, of occupying them themselves when there, but not of preventing others from taking possession of them in their absence. The dinners and other meals are, generally speaking, bad; not that there is not a plentiful supply, but that it is so difficult to supply seven hundred people sitting down in one room. In the morning, they all turn out from their little burrows, meet in the public walks, and go down to the springs before breakfast; during the forenoon, when it is too warm, they remain at home; after dinner they ride out or pay visits, and then end the day, either at the ball-room, or in little societies among one another. There is no want of handsome equipages, many four in hand (Virginia long tails) and every accommodation for these equipages. The crowd is very great, and it is astonishing what inconvenience people will submit to rather than not be accommodated somehow or another. Every cabin is like a rabbit burrow. In the one next to where I was lodged, in a room about fourteen feet square, and partitioned off as well as it could be, there slept a gentleman and his wife, his sister and brother, and a female servant. . . .

There is a sort of major-domo here, who regulates every department: his word is law, and his fiat immove-able, and he presumes not a little upon his power; a circumstance not to be surprised at, as he is as much courted and is as despotic as all the lady patronesses of Almacks rolled into one. He is called the Metternich of the mountains. No one is allowed accommodation at these springs who is not known, and generally speaking, only those families who travel in their private carriages. It is at this place that you feel how excessively aristocratical and exclusive the Americans would be, and indeed will be, in spite of their institutions. . . . Of course all the celebrated belles of the different States are to be met with here, as well as all the large fortunes, nor is there a scarcity of pretty and wealthy widows. The president, Mrs. Caton, the mother of Lady Wellesley, Lady Strafford, and Lady Caermarthen, the daughter of Carrol, of Carrolton, one of the real aristocracy of America, and a signer of the Declaration of Independence, and all the first old Virginian and Carolinia[n] families, many of them descendants of the old cavaliers, were at the springs when I arrived there; and I certainly must say that I never was at any watering-place in England where the company was so good and so select as at the Virginia springs in America. . . .

— Document No. 17 —

A MICHIGAN SCHOOLTEACHER IN MISSISSIPPI, 1858 [17]

In the fall of 1857, A. De Puy Van Buren left his home in Battle Creek, Michigan, and traveled by train and riverboat to the Yazoo Delta in search of a teaching position. He finally found one, early in 1858, near Yazoo City. His sojourn at Willow Dale plantation was an ingratiating moonlight and magnolia experience. He wrote "with perfect disregard to political prejudice, as if Slavery did not exist in our Southern Border." With poetic bent and many classical and literary allusions, he described idyllic life in a cotton plantation area. His scenes

[17] A. De Puy Van Buren, *Jottings of a Year's Sojourn in the South* (Battle Creek, Mich., 1859), pp. 159-171.

were "drawn coleur de rose" *from "impressions* coleur de nature."

✓   ✓   ✓

Willow Dale, so long my home on the Banks of the Yazoo, and where I have spent so many happy and delightful days, is truly a noble mansion and a very pleasant home. I lacked nothing now to make my sojourn in the South truly enjoyable. The pursuit after a school had been the *amari aliquid*—the drop of bitter—in my enjoyment here; that now had ceased, and I was prepared to commence my vocation, and enjoy Southern life. I had a very fine room furnished with everything to make one comfortable—a servant to build my fires, black my boots and do my errands. The family was a very pleasant one. And we had in addition to it, spending the winter with us, two fair cousins. . . .

Our evenings at Willow Dale were given to amusements. After one becomes acquainted with Southern life, he sees that society here must have them. In other lands, where life has a pursuit, less amusement is required. But here, where one finds its golden leisure, amusements are indispensable. The ladies of our household read, were fond of the works of literature and romance, and among authors they were very fond of SCOTT. He is a favorite of the South. Of the manners and scenes in his novels one is much reminded among this people. . . .

Besides reading, and the light work of the needle, our ladies gave their time to various pleasures—visiting and receiving visits, music, vocal and instrumental, the dance, cards, and *tete-a-tete*. Whist is universally acknowledged a lady's game. But euchre is the game of the South, and by choice, the Southern lady's game. . . .

We often had guests—ladies and gentlemen—from Yazoo city and other places, who sometimes would remain several days with us, and sometimes a planter's daughter would stay two or three weeks. Miss MOLLIE P., a charming young lady from Virginia, was with us a month or more during the winter. This made life at Willow Dale lively and interesting, and gave our evenings a greater fund of enjoyment.

Then we had moon-light sails on the noble Yazoo. I have no desire to disparage the North—my birth-place and home are there, and I love her. But there is a charm in Southern moon-light that I never before felt, that makes the night exceedingly lovely. . . .

Let us change the theme to our school. It certainly deserves a notice, if for no other reason than its being the termination of my adventures in the South. . . . There was no snow during the winter—nothing but a few disagreeable sleet-days, and when the walking was bad, which was made so by a little rain, I, if I chose, rode a-horse-back; steamers passing and repassing me, on my road to and from school. My friends, at home, would scarcely believe me, should I tell them that we had beautiful weather—warm and summer-like all January. During the spring and summer part of our school term, the water was so high in the Yazoo, that it overflowed the banks, and we sailed to school in a skiff—the scholars meeting at eight o'clock in the morning, under the willow-oak on the bank of the river, in front of Willow Dale, and a negro rowed us down-stream to the school-house, and came after us at night. . . .

Our Academy is within a stone's-throw, by the smallest scholar, of the Yazoo. The river rolls along in front of it. . . . It is built of gum-logs hewn square, and instead of being "chinked up," it is battened on the outside with cypress boards. It has two windows, one on each side. The door is in front, facing the river. It has a broad stone fire-place, at the opposite end, with a stick chimney running up on the outside. The floor is of smooth cypress boards. The one over head is of cypress-shakes laid from joist to joist, like battened-work. Two strips of desks are nailed against the wall, one on each side of the window, on one side; on the other side is a movable desk of cypress wood, for the teacher. Four chairs, with cow-hide bottoms, and one with a basket bottom, and three smaller ones for the small children, with several blocks of wood, sawed off chair-height, from a gum-log, are all the seats we had. There is a mantel-piece over the fire-place, and several pegs in the logs on the east side, to hang hats, bonnets and shawls on.

The house stands in a beautiful grove of willow-oaks,

and from their branches Southern birds sang their roundelays to us, all winter long. The gum tree, the persimmon, hackberry, and haw, were also near it. No hollies and magnolias were in sight. The long Spanish moss does not hang so thick from the trees in the valley, as in the up-lands; yet many of its floating tresses waved from the trees about our school-house.

My pupils were seven boys—intelligent, fine lads, three of whom were fourteen or fifteen years old, and two tiny damoiselles, one having a little black waiting maid, who attended her in school and out.

This was my school on commencing it; a month or two later we had three larger scholars. Their studies embraced Latin and the higher English branches. In history I never saw a class of scholars, of their age, that would equal them. I believe the South is ahead of us in giving attention to this study. Are not their Congressmen better informed in history than ours?

But to my school. Although we had the rogue, it is the only school I ever saw without a dunce in it. . . .

The advantage of teaching here, whether in the "old-field" schools—the common school South, or as tutor in a planter's family, or in the academies, is, you have a less number of scholars, and more *time* to devote to each study. The teacher has not got time, he cannot stop long enough by the way, North, to do anything like justice to the various branches he pretends to teach. . . .

We think the little Southron, on the whole, an interesting student, and we must say that we have ever been pleased with the deportment of children in planters' families; and it is a pleasure to walk along the streets in a Southern town, and witness the well-behaved conduct of children. You hear no swearing—no vulgar language. You see no vagrant boys—no wicked little urchins; nothing but the lively pranks and shouts and prattle of well-dressed children.

— Document No. 18 —

THE KENTUCKY RESOLUTIONS
OF 1799[18]

*Protests against the Alien and Sedition Acts of 1798
found expression the same year in the Kentucky and Virginia Resolutions, penned by Jefferson and Madison.
These were circulated to other state legislatures; and when
some replied unfavorably and others remained silent, the
Kentucky legislature issued a second set of resolutions
reaffirming its faith in the first and resolving further that
sovereign states had the right to nullify acts of Congress
that transcended congressional authority.*

✓   ✓   ✓

The representatives of the good people of this commonwealth, in General Assembly convened, having maturely considered the answers of sundry states in the
Union to their resolutions, passed the last session, respecting certain unconstitutional laws of Congress, commonly
called the Alien and Sedition Laws, would be faithless,
indeed, to themselves, and to those they represent, were
they silently to acquiesce in the principles and doctrines
attempted to be maintained in all those answers, that of
Virginia only excepted. To again enter the field of argument, and attempt more fully or forcibly to expose the
unconstitutionality of those obnoxious laws, would, it is
apprehended, be as unnecessary as unavailing. We cannot, however, but lament that, in the discussion of those
interesting subjects by sundry of the legislatures of our
sister states, unfounded suggestions and uncandid insin-

[18] From *The Debates in the several State Conventions on the
Adoption of the Federal Constitution,* by Jonathan
Elliot. Published by J. B. Lippincott Company (2nd ed.,
5 vols.; Philadelphia, 1888), IV, 544-545.

uations, derogatory to the true character and principles of this commonwealth, have been substituted in place of fair reasoning and sound argument. Our opinions of these alarming measures of the general government, together with our reasons for those opinions, were detailed with decency and with temper, and submitted to the discussion and judgment of our fellow-citizens throughout the Union. Whether the like decency and temper have been observed in the answers of most of those states who have denied or attempted to obviate, the great truths contained in those resolutions, we have now only to submit to a candid world. Faithful to the true principles of the federal Union, unconscious of any designs to disturb the harmony of that Union, and anxious only to escape the fangs of despotism, the good people of this commonwealth are regardless of censure or calumniation. Lest, however, the silence of this commonwealth should be construed into an acquiescence in the doctrines and principles advanced, and attempted to be maintained, by the said answers; or at least those of our fellow-citizens, throughout the Union, who so widely differ from us on those important subjects, should be deluded by the expectation that we shall be deterred from what we conceive our duty, or shrink from the principles contained in those resolutions,—therefore,

Resolved, That this commonwealth considers the federal Union, upon the terms and for the purposes specified in the late compact, conducive to the liberty and happiness of the several states: That it does now unequivocally declare its attachment to the Union, and to that compact, agreeably to its obvious and real intention, and will be among the last to seek its dissolution: That, if those who administer the general government be permitted to transgress the limits fixed by that compact, by a total disregard to the special delegations of power therein contained, an annihilation of the state governments, and the creation, upon their ruins, of a general consolidated government, will be the inevitable consequence: That the principle and construction, contended for by sundry of the state legislatures, that the general government is the exclusive judge of the extent of the powers delegated to it, stop not short of *despotism*—since the discretion of those who administer the government, and not the *Constitution*, would be the measure of their powers: That the several states who formed that instrument, being sovereign and independent, have the unquestionable right to judge of the infraction; and, *That a nullification by those sovereignties, of all unauthorized acts done under the color of that instrument, is the rightful remedy:* That this commonwealth does, under the most deliberate consideration, declare, that the said Alien and Sedition Laws are, in their opinion, palpable violations of the said Constitution; and, however cheerfully it may be disposed to surrender its opinion to a majority of its sister states, in matters of ordinary or doubtful policy, yet, in momentous regulations like the present, which so vitally wound the best rights of the citizen, it would consider a silent acquiescence as highly criminal: That, although this commonwealth, as a party to the federal compact, will bow to the laws of the Union, yet it does, at the same time, declare, that it will not now, or ever hereafter, cease to oppose, in a constitutional manner, every attempt, at what quarter soever offered, to violate that compact. And finally, in order that no pretext or arguments may be drawn from a supposed acquiescence, on the part of this commonwealth, in the constitutionality of those laws, and be thereby used as precedents for similar future violations of the federal compact—this commonwealth does now enter against them its solemn PROTEST.

— Document No. 19 —

CALHOUN'S FORT HILL LETTER ON STATE INTERPOSITION, 1832[19]

Calhoun was drawn reluctantly into the nullification controversy between the United States government and his state of South Carolina. Authorship of the South Carolina Exposition and Protest (1828), a statement of the doctrine of state interposition, was not widely recognized for some time. The Fort Hill Letter, addressed to Governor James Hamilton, Jr., August 28, 1832, was an open statement of the interposition theory that occupies forty-nine pages in Calhoun's Works.

✓   ✓   ✓

My dear Sir—I have received your note of the 31st July, requesting me to give you a fuller development of my views than that contained in my address last summer, on the right of a State to defend her reserved powers against the encroachments of the General Government. . . .

The formation and adoption of the Constitution are events so recent, and all the connected facts so fully attested, that it would seem impossible that there should be the least uncertainty in relation to them; and yet, judging by what is constantly heard and seen, there are few subjects on which the public opinion is more confused. . . . If by the people be meant the people collectively, and not the people of the several States taken separately; and if it be true, indeed, that the Constitution is the work of the American people collectively; if it originated

---

[19] Richard K. Cralle, ed., *The Works of John C. Calhoun* (6 vols.; New York, 1853), VI, 144-193, *passim.*

with them, and derives its authority from their will, then there is an end of the argument. The right claimed for a State of defending her reserved powers against the General Government, would be an absurdity. Viewing the American people collectively as a source of political power, the rights of the States would be mere concessions —concessions from the common majority, and to be revoked by them with the same facility that they were granted. The States would, on this supposition, bear to the Union the same relation that counties do to the States; and it would, in that case, be just as preposterous to discuss the right of interposition, on the part of a State, against the General Government, as that of the counties against the States themselves. That a large portion of the people of the United States thus regard the relation between the States and the General Government, including many who call themselves the friends of State-Rights and opponents of consolidation, can scarcely be doubted, as it is only on that supposition it can be explained that so many of that description should denounce the doctrine for which the State contends as so absurd. But, fortunately, the supposition is entirely destitute of truth. So far from the Constitution being the work of the American people collectively, no such political body either now or ever did exist. . . .

I will next proceed to state some of the results which necessarily follow from the facts which have been established.

The first, and, in reference to the subject of this communication, the most important, is, that there is *no direct* and *immediate* connection between the individual citizens of a State and the General Government. The relation between them is through the State. The Union is a union of States as communities, and not a union of individuals. . . . The Constitution was, accordingly, submitted to the States for their separate ratification; and it was only by the ratification by the State that its citizens became subject to the control of the General Government. . . . Another, and a highly important consequence, as regards the subject under investigation, follows with equal certainty; that, on a question whether a particular power exercised by the General Government be

granted by the Constitution, it belongs to the State as a
member of the Union, in her sovereign capactiy in convention, to determine definitively, as far as her citizens
are concerned, the extent of the obligation which she
contracted; and if, in her opinion, the act exercising the
power be unconstitutional, to declare it null and void,
which declaration would be obligatory on her citizens.
In coming to this conclusion, it may be proper to remark,
to prevent misrepresentation, that I do not claim for a
State the right to abrogate an act of the General Government. It is the Constitution that annuls an unconstitutional act. Such an act is of itself void and of no effect.
What I claim is, the right of the State, *as far as its citizens
are concerned, to declare the extent of the obligation, and
that such declaration is binding on them.* . . .

. . . I shall next proceed to consider the effects of such
declarations in reference to the General Government;
—a question which necessarily involves the consideration
of the relation between it and the States. . . . The
General Government is a case of joint agency—the joint
agent of the twenty-four sovereign States. It would be its
duty, according to the principles established in such cases,
instead of attempting to enforce its construction of its
powers against that of the States, to bring the subject before the States themselves . . . by a proposition to
amend, in the manner prescribed in the instrument, to be
acted on by them in the only mode they can, by expressly
granting or withholding the contested power. . . .

The construction which would confer on the Supreme
Court the power in question, rests on the ground that the
Constitution has conferred on that tribunal the high and
important right of deciding on the *constitutionality of
laws.* That it possesses this power I do not deny;—but I
do utterly that it is conferred by the Constitution either in
the provisions above cited, or any other. It is a power
derived from the necessity of the case; and, so far from
being possessed by the Supreme Court exclusively or
peculiarly, it not only belongs to every Court of the
country, high or low, civil or criminal, but to all foreign
Courts, before which a case may be brought involving the
construction of a law which may conflict with the provisions of the Constitution. . . .

The opinion that the General Government has the right to enforce its construction of its powers against a State in any mode whatever, is, in truth, founded on a fundamental misconception of our system. At the bottom of this, and, in fact, almost every other misconception as to the relation between the States and the General Government, lurks the radical error, that the latter is a national, and not, as in reality it is, a confederated Government; and that it derives its powers from a higher source than the States. . . .

I have now, I trust, conclusively shown that a State has a right, in her sovereign capacity, in convention, to declare an unconstitutional act of Congress to be null and void, and that such declarations would be obligatory on her citizens,—as highly so as the Constitution itself, —and conclusive against the General Government, which would have no right to enforce its construction of its powers against that of the State.

I next propose to consider the practical effect of the exercise of this high and important right—which, as the great conservative principle of our system, is known under the various names of nullification, interposition, and State veto—in reference to its operation viewed under different aspects: nullification,—as declaring null an unconstitutional act of the General Government, as far as the State is concerned; interposition,—as throwing the shield of protection between the citizens of a State and the encroachments of the Government; and veto,—as arresting or inhibiting its unauthorized acts within the limits of the State.

The practical effect, if the right was fully recognized, would be plain and simple, and has already, in a great measure, been anticipated. If the State has a right, there must, of necessity, be a corresponding obligation on the part of the General Government to acquiesce in its exercise; and, of course, it would be its duty to abandon the power, at least as far as the State is concerned,—to compromise the difficulty,—or apply to the States themselves, according to the form prescribed in the Constitution, to obtain the power by a grant. . . .

To suppose that force could be called in, implies, indeed, a great mistake both as to the nature of our Gov-

ernment and that of the controversy. It would be a legal
and constitutional contest—a conflict of moral, and not
physical force—a trial of constitutional, and not military
power,—to be decided before the judicial tribunals of the
country, and not on the field of battle. In such contest,
there would be no object for force, but those peaceful
tribunals—nothing on which it could be employed, but in
putting down courts and juries, and preventing the execution of judicial process. Leave these untouched, and
all the militia that could be called forth, backed by a regular force of ten times the number of our small, but gal-
lant and patriotic army, could have not the slightest effect
on the result of the controversy; but subvert these by an
armed body, and you subvert the very foundation of this
our free, constitutional, and legal system of government,
and rear in its place a military despotism. . . .

There is, indeed, one view, and one only, of the contest,
in which force could be employed; but that view, as between the parties, would supersede the Constitution itself:
—that nullification is secession,—and would, consequently, place the State, as to the others, in the relation
of a foreign state. Such, clearly, would be the effect of
secession; but it is equally clear that it would place the
State beyond the pale of all her federal relations, and,
thereby, all control on the part of the other States over
her. She would stand to them simply in the relation of
a foreign state, divested of all federal connection, and
having none other between them but those belonging to
the laws of nations. Standing thus towards one another,
force might, indeed, be employed against a State, but it
must be a belligerent force, preceded by a declaration of
war, and carried on with all its formalities. Such would be
the certain effect of secession; and if nullification be
secession—if it be but a different name for the same
thing—such, too, must be its effect; which presents the
highly important question, Are they, in fact, the
same? . . .

I shall now proceed to make good my assertion of their
total dissimilarity.

First, they are wholly dissimilar in their nature. *One
has reference to the parties themselves, and the other to
their agents*. Secession is a *withdrawal from the Union;*

a separation from *partners,* and, as far as depends on the member withdrawing, a *dissolution* of the partnership. It presupposes an association; a union of several States or individuals for a common object. Wherever these exist, secession may; and where they do not, it cannot. Nullification, on the contrary, *presupposes the relation of principal and agent:* the one granting a power to be executed,—the other, appointed by him with authority to execute it; *and is simply a declaration on the part of the principal, made in due form, that an act of the agent transcending his power is null and void.* . . .

The difference in their object is no less striking than in their nature. The object of secession is to *free* the withdrawing member from the *obligation* of the association or union, and is applicable to cases where the object of the association or union *has failed,* either by an abuse of power on the part of *its members,* or other causes. Its *direct and immediate object, as it concerns the withdrawing member, is the dissolution of the association or union,* as far as it is concerned. On the contrary, the object of nullification is to confine the agent within the limits of his powers, by arresting his acts transcending them, *not with the view of destroying the delegated or trust power, but to preserve it, by compelling the agent to fulfil the object for which the agency or trust was created; and is applicable only to cases where the trust or delegated powers are transcended on the part of the agent.* . . .

— Document No. 20 —

JEFFERSON ON EMANCIPATION AND COLONIZATION OF THE NEGRO, 1782[20]

After retiring from the governorship of the Old Dominion, Jefferson wrote, in 1781, his only book-length treatise, Notes on the State of Virginia, *which he "somewhat corrected and enlarged in the winter of 1782." The author of the Declaration's "free and equal" doctrine devoted a few pages to slavery and the Negro in his* Notes. *The Virginia liberal favored emancipation, but he was convinced freedmen should be colonized.*

To emancipate all slaves born after passing the act. The bill reported by the revisors does not inself contain this proposition; but an amendment containing it was prepared, to be offered to the legislature whenever the bill should be taken up, and further directing, that they should continue with their parents to a certain age, then be brought up, at the public expence, to tillage, arts or sciences, according to their geniuses, till the females should be eighteen, and the males twenty-one years of age, when they should be colonized to such place as the circumstances of the time should render most proper, sending them out with arms, implements of household and of the handicraft arts, seeds, pairs of the useful domestic animals, &c. to declare them a free and independant people, and extend to them our alliance and protection, till they have acquired strength; and to send vessels at the same time to other parts of the world for

[20] Thomas Jefferson, *Notes on the State of Virginia* (Philadelphia, 1801), pp. 267-269, 272, 280-282.

an equal number of white inhabitants; to induce whom to migrate hither, proper encouragements were to be proposed. It will probably be asked, Why not retain and incorporate the blacks into the state, and thus save the expence of supplying by importation of white settlers, the vacancies they will leave? Deep rooted prejudices entertained by the whites; ten thousand recollections, by the blacks, of the injuries they have sustained; new provocations; the real distinctions which nature has made; and many other circumstances, will divide us into parties, and produce convulsions, which will probably never end but in the extermination of the one or the other race.—To these objections, which are political, may be added others, which are physical and moral. . . . Comparing them by their faculties of memory, reason, and imagination, it appears to me that in memory they are equal to the whites; in reason much inferior, as I think one could scarcely be found capable of tracing and comprehending the investigations of Euclid; and that in imagination they are dull, tasteless, and anomalous. . . .

. . . The opinion, that they are inferior in the faculties of reason and imagination, must be hazarded with great diffidence. To justify a general conclusion, requires many observations, even where the subject may be submitted to the anatomical knife, to optical glasses, to analysis by fire, or by solvents. How much more than where it is a faculty, not a substance, we are examining; where it eludes the research of all the senses; where the conditions of its existence are various and variously combined; where the effects of those which are present or absent bid defiance to calculation; let me add too, as a circumstance of great tenderness, where our conclusion would degrade a whole race of men from the rank in the scale of beings which their Creator may perhaps have given them. To our reproach it must be said, that though for a century and a half we have had under our eyes the races of black and of red men, they have never yet been viewed by us as subjects of natural history. I advance it therefore as a suspicion only, that the blacks, whether originally a distinct race, or made distinct by time and circumstances, are inferior to the whites in the endowments both of body and mind. It is not against ex-

perience to suppose, that different species of the same
genus, or varieties of the same species, may possess different qualifications. Will not a lover of natural history
then, one who views the gradations in all the races of
animals with the eye of philosophy, excuse an effort to
keep those in the department of man as distinct as nature
has formed them? This unfortunate difference of colour,
and perhaps of faculty, is a powerful obstacle to the
emancipation of these people. Many of their advocates,
while they wish to vindicate the liberty of human nature
are anxious also to preserve its dignity and beauty. Some
of these, embarrassed by the question "What further is
to be done with them?" join themselves in opposition with
those who are actuated by sordid avarice only. Among
the Romans emancipation required but one effort. The
slave, when made free, might mix with, without stain-
ing the blood of his master. But with us a second is necessary, unknown to history. When freed, he is to be removed beyond the reach of mixture.

— Document No. 21 —

A PROSLAVERY ARGUMENT[21]

*In the years between 1832 and 1860, several
Southerners published formal defenses of slavery. James
H. Hammond, governor of South Carolina in the early
1840's and United States senator in the next decade,
replied to a British abolitionist, Thomas Clarkson, in two
long letters which appeared in print under the title,*

[21] E. N. Elliott, ed., *Cotton is King, and Pro-Slavery Arguments* (Augusta, Ga., 1860), pp. 646-648.

*"Slavery in the Light of Political Science." The following
paragraphs set forth Hammond's economic defense.*

✓   ✓   ✓

In an economical point of view—which I will not omit
—slavery presents some difficulties. As a general rule, I
agree it must be admitted, that free labor is cheaper
than slave labor. It is a fallacy to suppose that ours is
unpaid labor. The slave himself must be paid for, and thus
his labor is all purchased at once, and for no trifling sum.
His price was, in the first place, paid mostly to your countrymen, and assisted in building up some of those colossal
English fortunes, since illustrated by patents of nobility,
and splendid piles of architecture, stained and ce-
mented, if you like the expression, with the blood of kidnapped innocents; but loaded with no heavier curses
than abolition and its begotten fanaticisms have brought
upon your land—some of them fulfilled, some yet to be.
But besides the first cost of the slave, he must be fed and
clothed, well fed and well clothed, if not for humanity's
sake, that he may do good work, retain health and life,
and rear a family to supply his place. When old or sick,
he is clear expense, and so is the helpless portion of his
family. No poor law provides for him when unable to
work, or brings up his children for our service when we
need them. These are all heavy charges on slave labor.
Hence, in all countries where the denseness of the population has reduced it to a matter of perfect certainty,
that labor can be obtained, whenever wanted, and the
laborer be forced, by sheer necessity, to hire for the smallest pittance that will keep soul and body together, and
rags upon his back while in actual employment—dependent at all other times on alms or poor rates—in all such
countries it is found cheaper to pay this pittance, than to
clothe, feed, nurse, support through childhood, and pen-
sion in old age, a race of slaves. Indeed, the advantage is
so great as speedily to compensate for the loss of
the value of the slave. And I have no hesitation in saying,
that if I could cultivate my lands on these terms, I would,
without a word, resign my slaves, provided they could
be properly disposed of. But the question is, whether free
or slave labor is cheapest to us in this country, at this

time, situated as we are. And it is decided at once by the fact that we can not avail ourselves of any other than slave labor. We neither have, nor can we procure, other labor to any extent, or on any thing like the terms mentioned. We must, therefore, content ourselves with our dear labor, under the consoling reflection that what is lost to us, is gained to humanity; and that, inasmuch as our slave costs us more than your free men costs you, by so much is he better off. You will promptly say, emancipate your slaves, and then you will have free labor on suitable terms. That might be if there were five hundred where now there is one, and the continent, from the Atlantic to the Pacific, was as densely populated as your Island. But until that comes to pass, no labor can be procured in America on the terms you have it.

While I thus freely admit that to the individual proprietor slave labor is dearer than free, I do not mean to admit as equally clear that it is dearer to the community and to the State. Though it is certain that the slave is a far greater consumer than your laborer, the year round, yet your pauper system is costly and wasteful. Supported by your community at large, it is not administered by your hired agents with that interested care and economy —not to speak of humanity—which mark the management of ours, by each proprietor, for his own non-effectives; and is both more expensive to those who pay, and less beneficial to those who receive its bounties. Besides this, slavery is rapidly filling up our country with a hardy and healthy race, peculiarly adapted to our climate and productions, and conferring signal political and social advantages on us as a people, to which I have already referred.

THE PLANTATION OVERSEER: RULES AND REGULATIONS[22]

The overseer occupied a central position in plantation management. His annual contract was often accompanied by a set of rules for his guidance. The following "Rules for the Government and Management" of Plowdon C. J. Weston's several rice plantations was an elaborate body of regulations designed to promote the well-being of slaves as well as efficient management. Weston, like other Rice Coast planters, used the task system of labor as distinguished from the gang system used elsewhere in the South.

✓   ✓   ✓

The Proprietor, in the first place, wishes the Overseer most distinctly to understand that his first object is to be, under all circumstances, the care and well being of the negroes. The Proprietor is always ready to excuse such errors as may proceed from want of judgment; but he never can or will excuse any cruelty, severity, or want of care towards the negroes. For the well being, however, of the negroes, it is absolutely necessary to maintain obedience, order, and discipline; to see that the tasks are punctually and carefully performed, and to conduct the business steadily and firmly, without weakness on the one hand, or harshness on the other. For such ends the following regulations have been instituted. . . .

Allowance—Food.—Great care should be taken that the negroes should never have less than their regular allowance: in all cases of doubt, it should be

[22] Reprinted by permission of the publishers, The Arthur H. Clark Company, from *Plantation and Frontier*, ed. by Ulrich B. Phillips (2 vols.; Cleveland, 1910), I, 116-122.

given in favor of the largest quantity. The measures should not be *struck,* but rather heaped up over. None but provisions of the best quality should be used. If any is discovered to be damaged, the Proprietor, if at hand, is to be immediately informed; if absent, the damaged article is to be destroyed. The corn should be carefully winnowed before grinding. The small rice is apt to become sour: as soon as this is perceived it should be given out every meal until finished, or until too sour to be used, when it should be destroyed.

Work, Holidays, Ec.—No work on any sort or kind is to be permitted to be done by negroes on Good Friday, or Christmas day, or on any Sunday, except going for a Doctor, or nursing sick persons; any work of this kind done on any of these days is to be reported to the Proprietor, who will pay for it. The two days following Christmas day; the first Saturdays after finishing threshing, planting, hoeing, harvest, are also to be holidays, on which the people may work for themselves. Only half task is to be done on every Saturday, except during planting and harvest, and those who had misbehaved or been lying up during the week. A task is as much work as the meanest full hand can do in nine hours, working industriously. The Driver is each morning to point out to each hand their task, and this task is never to be increased, and no work is to be done over task except under the most urgent necessity, which overwork is to be reported to the Proprietor, who will pay for it. No negro is to be put into a task which they cannot finish with tolerable ease. . . .

*Punishme*nts—It is desirable to allow 24 hours to elapse between the discovery of the offence, and the punishment. No punishment is to exceed 15 lashes: in cases where the Overseer supposes a severer punishment necessary, he must apply to the Proprietor, or to ————, Esq., in case of the Proprietor's absence from the neighborhood. Confinement (not in the stocks) is to be preferred to whipping: but the stoppage of Saturday's allowance, and doing whole task on Saturday, will suffice to prevent ordinary offences. Special care must be taken to prevent any indecency in punishing women. No Driver, or other negro, is to be allowed to punish any person in any way, except by order of the Overseer, and in his presence. . . .

Sickness—All sick persons are to stay in the hospital night and day, from the time they first complain to the time they are able to go to work again. The nurses are to be responsible for the sick not leaving the house, and for the cleanliness of the bedding, utensils, &c. The nurses are never to be allowed to give any medicine without the orders of the Overseer or Doctor. A woman, beside the plantation nurse, must be put to nurse all persons seriously ill. In all cases at all serious the Doctor is to be sent for, and his orders are to be strictly attended to; no alteration is to be made in the treatment he directs. Lying-in women are to be attended by the midwife as long as is necessary, and by a woman put to nurse them for a fortnight. They will remain at the negro houses for 4 weeks, and then will work 2 weeks on the highland. In some cases, however, it is necessary to allow them to lie up longer. . . .

Duties of Officials.—Drivers are, under the Overseer, to maintain discipline and order on the place. They are to be responsible for the quiet of the negro-houses, for the proper performance of tasks, for bringing out the people early in the morning, and generally for the immediate inspection of such things as the Overseer only generally superintends. For other duties of Driver, see article Work.

Watchmen are to be responsible for the safety of the buildings, boats, flats, and fences, and that no cattle or hogs come inside the place. If he perceives any buildings or fences out of repair, or if he hears of any robberies or trespasses, he must immediately give the Overseer notice. He must help to kill hogs and beeves.

Trunk-minders undertake the whole care of the trunks, [i.e., sluice-valves] under the Proprietor's and Overseer's directions. Each has a boat to himself, which he must on no account let any body else use.

Nurses are to take care of the sick, and to be responsible for the fulfilment of the orders of the Overseer, or Doctor, (if he is in attendance.) The food of the sick will be under their charge. They are expected to keep the hospital floors, bedding, blankets, utensils, &c., in perfect cleanliness. Wood should be allowed them. Their assistants should be entirely under their control. When the Proprietor and Overseer are absent, and a serious case occurs, the nurse is to send for the Doctor.

Yard Watchman is responsible for the crop in the yard, and for the barns.

Cooks take every day the provisions for all the people, the sick only excepted, (see article *Allowance*.) The Overseer is particularly requested to see that they cook cleanly and well. One cook cooks on the Island, the other on the Main, for the carpenters, millers, highland hands, &c. . . .

Miscellaneous Observations.—The Proprietor wishes particularly to impress on the Overseer the criterions by which he will judge of his usefulness and capacity. *First*—by the general well-being of all the negroes; their cleanly appearance, respectful manners, active and vigorous obedience; their completion of their tasks well and early; the small amount of punishment; the excess of births over deaths; the small number of persons in hospital, and the health of the children. *Secondly*—the condition and fatness of the cattle and mules; the good repair of all the fences and buildings, harness, boats, flats, and ploughs; more particularly the good order of the banks and trunks, and the freedom of the fields from grass and volunteer. *Thirdly*—the amount and quality of the rice and provision crops. The Overseer will fill up the printed forms sent to him every week, from which the Proprietor will obtain most of the facts he desires, to form the estimate mentioned above.

The Overseer is expressly prohibited from three things viz: bleeding, giving spirits to any negro without a Doctor's order, and letting any negro on the place have or keep any gun, powder, or shot. . . .

Women with six children alive at any *one* time, are allowed all Saturday to themselves.

Fighting, particularly amongst women, and obscene, or abusive language, is to be always vigorously punished.

During the summer, fresh spring water must be carried every day on the Island. Anybody found drinking ditch or river water must be punished.

Finally.—The Proprietor hopes the Overseer will remember that a system of strict justice is necessary to good management. No person should ever be allowed to break a law without being punished, or any person punished who has not broken a well known law. Every person should be made perfectly to understand what they are punished for, and should be made to perceive that they are not punished in anger, or through caprice. All abusive language or violence of demeanor should be avoided: they reduce the man who uses them to a level with a negro, and are hardly ever forgotten by those to whom they are addressed.

— Document No. 23 —

A FREE NEGRO RECALLS HIS LIFE IN SLAVERY [23]

Frederick, Douglass, christened Frederick Augustus Washington Bailey, escaped from slavery probably at the age of twenty-one. He became an effective antislavery organizer, lecturer, and newspaper editor. In 1845 Douglass published an autobiographical Narrative; *many years later a* Life *and* Times *from which the following excerpt of experiences in slavery is drawn.*

✔   ✔   ✔

I have already implied that Mr. Edward Covey was a poor man. He was, in fact, just beginning to lay the foundation of his fortune, as fortune was regarded in a slave state. The first condition of wealth and respectabil-

[23] *Life and Times of Frederick Douglass, Written by Himself* (Hartford, 1882), pp. 138-140.

ity there being the ownership of human property, every nerve was strained by the poor man to obtain it, with little regard sometimes as to the means. In pursuit of this object, pious as Mr. Covey was, he proved himself as unscrupulous and base as the worst of his neighbors. In the beginning he was only able—as he said—"to buy one slave;" and scandalous and shocking as is the fact, he boasted that he bought her simply "as a breeder." But the worst of this is not told in this naked statement. This young woman (Caroline was her name) was virtually compelled by Covey to abandon herself to the object for which he had purchased her; and the result was the birth of twins at the end of the year. At this addition to his human stock Covey and his wife were ecstatic with joy. No one dreamed of reproaching the woman or of finding fault with the hired man, Bill Smith, the father of the children, for Mr. Covey himself had locked the two up together every night, thus inviting the result.

But I will pursue this revolting subject no farther. No better illustration of the unchaste, demoralizing, and debasing character of slavery can be found, than is furnished in the fact that his professedly Christian slave-holder, amidst all his prayers and hymns, was shame-lessly and boastfully encouraging and actually compelling, in his own house, undisguised and unmitigated fornica-tion, as a means of increasing his stock. It was the *system* of slavery which made this allowable, and which con-demned the slaveholder for buying a slave woman and devoting her to this life, no more than for buying a cow and raising stock from her, and the same rules were ob-served, with a view to increasing the number and quality of the one, as of the other.

If at any one time in my life, more than another, I was made to drink the bitterest dregs of slavery, that time was during the first six months of my stay with this man Covey. We were worked all weathers. It was never too hot, or too cold; it could never rain, blow, snow, or hail too hard for us to work in the field. Work, work, work, was scarcely more than the order of the day than of the night. The longest days were too short for him, and the shortest nights were too long for him. I was some-what unmanageable at the first, but a few months of this discipline tamed me. Mr. Covey succeeded in *breaking* me—in body, soul, and spirit. My natural elasticity was crushed; my intellect languished; the disposition to read departed, the cheerful spark that lingered about my eye died out; the dark night of slavery closed in upon me, and behold a man transformed to a brute!

Sunday was my only leisure time. I spent this in a sort of beast-like stupor, between sleeping and waking, under some large tree. At times I would rise up, a flash of energetic freedom would dart through my soul, accompanied with a faint beam of hope that flickered for a moment, and then vanished. I sank down again, mourning over my wretched condition. I was sometimes tempted to take my life and that of Covey, but was prevented by a combination of hope and fear. My sufferings, as I remember them now, seem like a dream rather than a stern reality.

Our house stood within a few rods of the Chesapeake bay, whose broad bosom was ever white with sails from every quarter of the habitable globe. Those beautiful vessels, robed in white, and so delightful to the eyes of freemen, were to me so many shrouded ghosts, to terrify and torment me with thoughts of my wretched condition. I have often, in the deep stillness of a summer's Sabbath, stood all alone on the noble banks of that bay, and traced, with saddened heart and tearful eye, the countless number of sails moving off to the mighty ocean. The sight of these always affected me powerfully. My thoughts would compel utterance; and there, with no audience but the Almighty, I would pour out my soul's complaint in my rude way with an apostrophe to the moving multitude of ships.

— Document No. 24 —

THE GEORGIA PLATFORM
OF 1850[24]

Southern extremists at mid-century thought the time propitious for disruption of the Union and the formation of a separate confederacy. Clay's compromise measures of 1850 gave moderates an opportunity to quiet discontent and to seek redress of grievances under the Constitution. The Georgia Platform, framed by a convention called to consider the state's relationship with the Union, expressed the conditions under which its continuation would be feasible.

/　　　　　/　　　　　/

To the end that the position of this State may be clearly apprehended by her Confederates of the South and of the North, and that she may be blameless of all future consequences—

Be it resolved by the people of Georgia in Convention assembled, First. That we hold the American Union second in importance only to the rights and principles it was designed to perpetuate. That past associations, present fruition, and future prospects, will bind us to it so long as it continues to be the safe-guard of those rights and principles.

Second. That if the thirteen original Parties to the Compact, bordering the Atlantic in a narrow belt, while their separate interests were in embryo, their peculiar tendencies scarcely developed, their revolutionary trials and triumphs still green in memory found Union impossible without compromise, the thirty-one of this

[24] Alexander H. Stephens, *A Constitutional View of the Late War Between the States* (2 vols.; Philadelphia, 1868-1870), II, Appendix B, 676-677.

day may well yield somewhat in the conflict of opinion and policy, to preserve that Union which has extended the sway of Republican Government over a vast wilderness to another ocean, and proportionally advanced their civilization and national greatness.

Third. That in this spirit the State of Georgia has maturely considered the action of Congress, embracing a series of measures for the admission of California into the Union, the organization of Territorial Governments for Utah and New Mexico, the establishment of a boundary between the latter and the State of Texas, the suppression of the slave-trade in the District of Columbia, and the extradition of fugitive slaves, and (connected with them) the rejection of propositions to exclude slavery from the Mexican Territories, and to abolish it in the District of Columbia; and, whilst she does not wholly approve, will abide by it as a permanent adjustment of this sectional controversy.

Fourth. That the State of Georgia, in the judgment of this Convention, will and ought to resist, even (as a last resort) to a disruption of every tie which binds her to the Union, any future Act of Congress abolishing Slavery in the District of Columbia, without the consent and petition of the slave-holders thereof, or any Act abolishing Slavery in places within the slave-holding States, purchased by the United States for the erection of forts, magazines, arsenals, dock-yards, navy-yards, and other like purposes; or in any Act suppressing the slave-trade between slave-holding States; or in any refusal to admit as a State any Territory applying, because of the existence of Slavery therein; or in any Act prohibiting the introduction of slaves into the Territories of Utah and New Mexico; or in any Act repealing or materially modifying the laws now in force for the recovery of fugitive slaves.

Fifth. That it is the deliberate opinion of this Convention, that upon the faithful execution of the Fugitive Slave Bill by the proper authorities, depends the preservation of our much loved Union.

— Document No. 25 —

HELPER INDICTS SLAVERY, 1857[25]

Hinton R. Helper's Impending Crisis of the South *(1857), read widely in the North, infuriated many Southerners. Two years after his work appeared, he published a briefer edition.* A Compendium of Helper's Impending Crisis of the South. *Republican members of Congress, including John Sherman, candidate for the speakership in 1859, circulated it under the congressional frank in preparation for the campaign of 1860. There was considerable truth in what Helper wrote despite much distortion of economic statistics.*

The North is the Mecca of our merchants, and to it they must and do make two pilgrimages per annum— one in the spring and one in the fall. All our commercial, mechanical, manufactural, and literary supplies come from there. We want Bibles, brooms, buckets and books, and we go to the North; we want pens, ink, paper, wafers and envelopes, and we go to the North; we want shoes, hats, handkerchiefs, unbrellas and pocket knives, and we go to the North; we want furniture, crockery, glassware and pianos, and we go to the North; we want toys, primers, school books, fashionable apparel, machinery, medicines, tombstones, and a thousand other things, and we go to the North for them all. Instead of keeping our money in circulation at home, by patronizing our own mechanics, manufacturers, and laborers, we send it all away to the North, and there it remains; it never falls into our hands again.

[25] Hinton Rowan Helper, *The Impending Crisis of the South: How To Meet It* (New York, 1857), pp. 21-25.

In one way or another we are more or less subservient to the North every day of our lives. In infancy we are swaddled in Northern muslin; in childhood we are humored with Northern gewgaws; in youth we are instructed out of Northern books; at the age of maturity we sow our "wild oats" on Northern soil; in middle-life we exhaust our wealth, energies and talents in the dishonorable vocation of entailing our dependence on our children and on our children's children, and, to the neglect of our own interests and the interests of those around us, in giving aid and succor to every department of Northern power; in the decline of life we remedy our eye-sight with Nothern spectacles, and support our infirmities with Northern canes; in old age we are drugged with Northern physic; and, finally, when we die, our inanimate bodies, shrouded in Northern cambric, are stretched upon the bier, borne to the grave in a Northern carriage, entombed with Northern spade, and memorized with a Northern slab! . . .

And now to the point. In our opinion, an opinion which has been formed from data obtained by assiduous researches, and comparisons, from laborious investigation, logical reasoning, and earnest reflection, the causes which have impeded the progress and prosperity of the South, which have dwindled our commerce, and other similar pursuits, into the most contemptible insignificance; sunk a large majority of our people into galling poverty and ignorance, rendered a small minority conceited and tyrannical, and driven the rest away from their homes; entailed upon us a humiliating dependence on the Free States; disgraced us in the recesses of our own souls, and brought us under reproach in the eyes of all civilized and enlightened nations—may all be traced to one common source, and there find solution in the most hateful and horrible word, that was ever incorporated into the vocabulary of human economy—*Slavery!*

— Document No. 26 —

A VIRGINIA REPLY TO HELPER'S "IMPENDING CRISIS," 1860[26]

A Virginian, Samuel M. Wolfe, thought Helper's Im-pending Crisis "too contemptible to notice," but the Republican party's use of the Compendium *induced him to reply to the "vile wretch." He "dissected" the North Carolinian's statistical analyses to aid Northern and Southern "patriots" in defeating "HELPERISM AND SHERMANISM." "Wolfe's book is a good illustration of Southern polemics that equaled Helper's distortion of figures and surpassed his offensive language.*

✓ ✓ ✓

With such manifest unfairness, as the analysis of the statistics which we have here given shows, it would war-rant the suspicion and belief that this "Helper Book," like most of the arguments of the leading "Black Repub-licans," is a mere cunningly devised compilation of spirited extracts from sundry speeches, messages, etc., of prominent men, and forced statistics, gotten up de-signedly to inflame and mislead the Northern masses.

The exportable products of the fifteen Slave States amount annually to $270,000,000 exclusive of gold and foreign merchandise re-exported; and their annual de-mand for the productions of other countries is about $225,000,000. There are 80,000 cotton plantations in the South, and the aggregate value of their annual prod-ucts is $128,000,000. There are 16,000 tobacco planta-tions, and their annual products amount to $15,000,000. There are 2,600 sugar plantations, the products of which average annually $13,000,000. There are 700 rice plan-

[26] Samuel M. Wolfe, *Helper's Impending Crisis Dissected* (Philadelphia, 1860), pp. 38-43.

tations, which yield annually a revenue of $6,000,000. Breadstuffs and provisions yield $78,000,000; the products of the forest amount to $10,700,000; manufactures yield $31,000,000; and the products of the sea yield $3,356,000; exclusive of $30,000,000 we send to the North!

These facts and figures rest mostly upon the authority of the *Southern Cultivator, De Bow's Review,* and the speeches in Congress of Senator Hammond, and Hon. L. M. Keitt, M. C. of South Carolina. But we are happy to find them sustained by the Secretary of the Treasury, in a late Report; and laid before Congress by "His Excellency President Buchanan," and by him endorsed.

— Document No. 27 —

THE SOUTHERN DEMOCRATIC PLATFORM, 1860[27]

After withdrawing from the national convention of the Democratic party at Charleston, lower South delegates, with some accretions from the other Southern states, adjourned to Baltimore where Douglas Democrats had scheduled another meeting. There Southern Democrats adopted a platform and nominated John C. Breckinridge of Kentucky for president and Joseph Lane of Oregon for vice-president. A later convention of this "National Democratic party" at Richmond ratified what Southern Democrats had done at Baltimore.

✦   ✦   ✦

Resolved, That the platform adopted by the Demo-

[27] Kirk H. Porter, comp., *National Party Platforms* (New York, 1924), pp. 54-55. Copyright 1924 by the Macmillan Company. Used with permission.

cratic party at Cincinnati [1856] be affirmed, with the
following explanatory resolutions:

1. That the Government of a Territory organized
by an act of Congress is provisional and temporary,
and during its existence all citizens of the United States
have an equal right to settle with their property in the
Territory, without their rights, either of person or property, being destroyed or impaired by Congressional or
Territorial legislation.

2. That it is the duty of the Federal Government,
in all its departments, to protect, when necessary, the
rights of persons and property in the Territories, and
wherever else its constitutional authority extends.

3. That when the settlers in a Territory, having an
adequate population, form a State Constitution, the right
of sovereignty commences, and being consummated by
admission into the Union, they stand on an equal foot-
ing with the people of other States, and the State thus
organized ought to be admitted into the Federal Union,
whether its Constitution prohibits or recognizes the institution of slavery.

Resolved, That the Democratic party are in favor of
the acquisition of the Island of Cuba, on such terms as
shall be honorable to ourselves and just to Spain, at the
earliest practicable moment.

Resolved, That the enactments of State Legislatures
to defeat the faithful execution of the Fugitive Slave Law
are hostile in character, subversive of the Constitution,
and revolutionary in their effect.

Resolved, That the Democarcy of the United States
recognize it as the imperative duty of this Government
to protect the naturalized citizen in all his rights, whether
at home or in foreign lands, to the same extent as its
native-born citizens.

WHEREAS, One of the greatest necessities of the
age, in a political, commercial, postal and military point
of view, is a speedy communication between the Pacific
and Atlantic coasts. Therefore be it

Resolved, That the National Democratic party do
hereby pledge themselves to use every means in their
power to secure the passage of some bill, to the extent
of the constitutional authority of Congress, for the con-

struction of a Pacific Railroad from the Mississippi River to the Pacific Ocean, at the earliest practicable moment.

A SHORT BIBLIOGRAPHY

Alden, John R., *The South in the Revolution, 1763-1789* (Baton Rouge, 1957).

Bancroft, Frederic, *Slave-Trading in the Old South* (Baltimore, 1931).

Barnes, Gilbert H., *The Antislavery Impulse, 1830-1844* (New York, 1933).

Bassett, John S., *The Southern Plantation Overseer as Revealed in His Letters* (Northampton, 1925).

Bridenbaugh, Carl, *Myths and Realities; Societies in the Colonial South* (Baton Rouge, 1952).

Carpenter, Jesse T., *The South as a Conscious Minority, 1789-1861* (New York, 1930).

Cash, Wilbur J., *The Mind of the South* (New York, 1941).

Cotterill, Robert S., *The Old South* (Glendale, Calif., 1936).

Coulter, E. Merton, *College Life in the Old South* (New York, 1928).

Craven, Avery O., *The Coming of the Civil War* (New York, 1942).

Craven, Avery O., *The Growth of Southern Nationalism, 1848-1861* (Baton Rouge, 1953).

Craven, Wesley F., *The Southern Colonies in the Seventeenth Century, 1607-1689* (Baton Rouge, 1949).

Dodd, William E., *The Cotton Kingdom* (New Haven, 1919).

Dumond, Dwight L., *Antislavery Origins of the Civil War in the United States* (Ann Arbor, 1939).

Eaton, Clement, *A History of the Old South* (New York, 1949).

Frankin, John H., *The Militant South, 1800-1861* (Cambridge, Mass., 1956).

Gaines, Francis P., *The Southern Plantation; A Study in the Development and the Accuracy of a Tradition* (New York, 1925).

Gray, Lewis C., *History of Agriculture in the Southern United States to 1860*, 2 vols. (Washington, 1933).

Hesseltine, William B., *The South in American History* (New York, 1943).

Johnson, Thomas C., Jr., *Scientific Interests in the Old South* (New York, 1936).

Nevins, Allan, *The Emergence of Lincoln*, 2 vols. (New York, 1950).

Owsley, Frank L., *Plain People of the Old South* (Baton Rouge, 1949).

Phillips, Ulrich B., *The Course of the South to Secession* (New York, 1939).

Phillips, Ulrich B., *Life and Labor in the Old South* (Boston, 1929).

Simkins, Francis B., *A History of the South* (New York, 1953).

Stampp, Kenneth M., *The Peculiar Institution; Slavery in the Ante-Bellum South* (New York, 1956).

Stephenson, Wendell H. *Isaac Franklin, Slave Trader and Planter of the Old South* (Baton Rouge, 1938).

Sydnor, Charles S., *The Development of Southern Sectionalism, 1819-1848* (Baton Rouge, 1948).

Thorp, Willard, *A Southern Reader* (New York, 1955).

Van Noppen, Ina W., *The South; A Documentary History* (Princeton, 1958).

Vance, Rupert B., *The Human Geography of the South* (Chapel Hill, 1932).

Wertenbaker, Thomas J., *The Old South; The Founding of American Civilization* (New York, 1942).

Wertenbaker, Thomas J., *The Planters of Colonial Virginia* (Princeton, 1922).

Wright, Louis B., *The First Gentlemen of Virginia: Intellectual Qualities of the Early Colonial Ruling Class* (San Marino, 1940).

INDEX

1 *MAKING OF MODERN FRENCH MIND*—Kohn
2 *THE AMERICAN REVOLUTION*—Morris
3 *THE LATE VICTORIANS*—Ausubel
4 *WORLD IN THE 20th CENTURY*—Rev. Ed. Snyder
5 *50 DOCUMENTS OF THE 20th CENTURY*—Snyder
6 *THE AGE OF REASON*—Snyder
7 *MARX AND THE MARXISTS*—Hook
8 *NATIONALISM*—Kohn
9 *MODERN JAPAN*—Rev. Ed. Tiedemann
10 *50 DOCUMENTS OF THE 19th CENTURY*—Snyder
11 *CONSERVATISM*—Viereck
12 *THE PAPACY*—Corbett
13 *AGE OF THE REFORMATION*—Bainton
14 *DOCUMENTS IN AMERICAN HISTORY*—Rev. Ed. Morris
15 *CONTEMPORARY AFRICA*—Rev. Ed. Wallbank
16 *THE RUSSIAN REVOLUTIONS OF 1917*—Curtiss
17 *THE GREEK MIND*—Agard
18 *BRITISH CONSTITUTIONAL HISTORY SINCE 1832*—Schuyler and Weston
19 *THE NEGRO IN THE U.S.*—Logan
20 *AMERICAN CAPITALISM*—Hacker
21 *LIBERALISM*—Schapiro
22 *THE FRENCH REVOLUTION, 1789-1799*—Gershoy
23 *HISTORY OF MODERN GERMANY*—Snyder
24 *HISTORY OF MODERN RUSSIA*—Kohn
25 *NORTH ATLANTIC CIVILIZATION*—Kraus
26 *NATO*—Salvadori
27 *DOCUMENTS IN U.S. FOREIGN POLICY*—Brockway
28 *AMERICAN FARMERS' MOVEMENTS*—Shannon
29 *HISTORIC DECISIONS OF SUPREME COURT*—Swisher
30 *MEDIEVAL TOWN*—Mundy and Riesenberg
31 *REVOLUTION AND REACTION 1848-1852*—Bruun
32 *SOUTHEAST ASIA AND WORLD TODAY*—Buss
33 *HISTORIC DOCUMENTS OF W. W. I*—Snyder
34 *HISTORIC DOCUMENTS OF W. W. II*—Langsam
35 *ROMAN MIND AT WORK*—MacKendrick
36 *SHORT HISTORY OF CANADA*—Masters
37 *WESTWARD MOVEMENT IN U.S.*—Billington
38 *DOCUMENTS IN MEDIEVAL HISTORY*—Downs
39 *HISTORY OF AMERICAN BUSINESS*—Cochran
40 *DOCUMENTS IN CANADIAN HISTORY*—Talman
41 *FOUNDATIONS OF ISRAEL*—Janowsky
42 *MODERN CHINA*—Rowe
43 *BASIC HISTORY OF OLD SOUTH*—Stephenson
44 *THE BENELUX COUNTRIES*—Eyck
45 *MEXICO AND THE CARIBBEAN*—Rev. Ed. Hanke
46 *SOUTH AMERICA*—Rev. Ed. Hanke
47 *SOVIET FOREIGN POLICY, 1917-1941*—Kennan
48 *THE ERA OF REFORM, 1830-1860*—Commager
49 *EARLY CHRISTIANITY*—Bainton
50 *RISE AND FALL OF THE ROMANOVS*—Mazour
51 *CARDINAL DOCUMENTS IN BRITISH HISTORY*—Schuyler and Weston
52 *HABSBURG EMPIRE 1804-1918*—Kohn
53 *CAVOUR AND UNIFICATION OF ITALY*—Salvadori
54 *ERA OF CHARLEMAGNE*—Easton and Wieruszowski
55 *MAJOR DOCUMENTS IN AMERICAN ECONOMIC HISTORY, Vol. I*—Hacker
56 *MAJOR DOCUMENTS IN AMERICAN ECONOMIC HISTORY, Vol. II*—Hacker
57 *HISTORY OF THE CONFEDERACY*—Vandiver
58 *COLD WAR DIPLOMACY*—Graebner
59 *MOVEMENTS OF SOCIAL DISSENT IN MODERN EUROPE*—Schapiro
60 *MEDIEVAL COMMERCE*—Adelson
61 *THE PEOPLE'S REPUBLIC OF CHINA*—Buss
62 *WORLD COMMUNISM*—Hook
63 *ISLAM AND THE WEST*—Hitti